THE MASTER-MYTH OF MODERN SOCIETY

A Sketch of the Scientific Worldview and Its Psycho-social Effects

G. Marian Kinget

University Press of America,® Inc.
Lanham • New York • Oxford

Copyright © 2000 by
University Press of America,® Inc.
4720 Boston Way
Lanham, Maryland 20706

12 Hid's Copse Rd.
Cumnor Hill, Oxford OX2 9JJ

Library of Congress Cataloging-in-Publication Data

Kinget, G. Marian
The master-myth of modern society : a sketch of the scientific
Worldview and its psycho-social effects / G. Marian Kinget.
p. cm.
Includes bibliographical references.
1. Psychoanalysis. 2. Myth—Psychological aspects. I. Title
RC506.K525 1999 150.19—dc21 99-051511 CIP

ISBN 0-7618-1570-8 (pbk: alk. ppr.)

∞™ The paper used in this publication meets the minimum
requirements of American National Standard for Information
Sciences—Permanence of Paper for Printed Library Materials,
ANSI Z39.48—1984

CONTENTS

PART THREE

PART FOUR

What is the work of works for man if not to establish,
in and by each one of us, an absolutely original
center in which the universe reflects itself
in a unique and inimitable way?

— Teilhard de Chardin,
The Phenomenon of Man

FOREWORD

The year before Dr. G. Marian Kinget came to America, the eminent American philosopher, Mortimer J. Adler, called for a *Summa Dialectica* aiming at

> the renewal of the intellectual community...[and the beginning formulation of] the dialectical unity and dialectical truth which resides in the whole tradition of learning and thought; which must be there implicitly, awaiting explication, if for no other reason, because that tradition is the expression of the human mind, common to all men of every time and place, living in a common world....[Such a *Summa*] must provide the intellectual pattern of a world community, the common medium of exchange for all mankind, not only living together in one world at last, but also able to think together in a single universe of discourse.[1]

In 1948 Dr. Kinget, a native of Belgium, educated in traditional European systems from the early to the mid-20th century, arrived in the United States after surviving World War II and completing her Ph.D. Her experiences here, first as a post-doctoral student in Psychology, and then as professor and psychotherapist, led her to observe almost thirty years later:

"America: We have all the ingredients of the Good Life but we are also singularly unenlightened about the human condition."[2] "Introduction to man's nature, his history and destiny, is skimpy when not altogether lacking" in the schooling received in preparation for living in today's technological society.[3]

That was 25 years ago.

This June 1999, compelled by the same concerns, the Library of Congress in Washington, D.C. hosted an international symposium, "Frontiers of the Mind in the 21st Century," where scholars gathered to discuss "the state of knowledge in our time…[when] specialization and caution, professionally and politically inspired, have taken their toll on intellectual discourse."[4] "My concern," said James H. Billington, Librarian of Congress, "is that the academic enterprise in America is incessantly preoccupied with giving definitive answers to trivial questions instead of tentative answers to important ones."[5]

Prime among the "important questions" is the question of the nature of the human being—a question that has divided "not merely the tradition of psychology, but the whole tradition of Western thought."[6] It is within this particular and timeless discussion that the late Professor Kinget found a spiritual niche and engagement for a lifetime.

Urged once to write an autobiography, Professor Kinget replied, "It would be only a skeleton." So, we don't have the biography that only she could have written. We do, however, have some parts of that "skeleton," or the facts without their lived or existential meaning.

Born in 1910 in Steenkerke, Belgium, the youngest, by several years, of four children, she spent much time alone and much of that time freely wandering the fields and streams of the countryside near the family farm. From this idyllic childhood, she developed a profound love of solitude and natural beauty that stayed with her throughout the rest of her life. Yet, even this enviably simple time gave rise to unpleasant memories of terrible sounds at night coming from the trenches in France during World War I, and a first sense of loss at the death of a young French soldier who had befriended her while being housed by the family. The death of her father when she was nine years old had, in addition to the natural personal effects, far-reaching practical and social consequences in that culture at that time, where masculine privilege prevailed.

In her teens, she went to boarding school in England, where she added another of the five languages in which she was fluent as an adult. Later, harkening back to the practice of earlier centuries and the "grand tour," she traveled Europe for several years as a "free student" auditing classes in a number of countries, visiting friends and discovering new places; she counted these travels among the most enjoyable of times. It was during one of those trips that the bells literally began to toll signalling the start of World War II and the need to return home.

She spoke infrequently of her experiences in Belgium and France during the war; but we do know of the lack of food supplies; of hiding French soldiers in the attic; of bomb shelters and bombardments; and that she was among those fleeing the German advance at the Battle of Dunkirk, appalled at people going past in cars loaded with material possessions, while neighbors retreated on foot.

She received most of her formal education during the war years. In 1940, she earned a Master of Science Degree in Social Work from the School of Social Work in Brussels. While there, her incisive questioning also earned her the label, "esprit critique!" and apparently drew the attention of more sympathetic minds, because she was encouraged, and allowed, to enter the University of Louvain without the Greek language admission prerequisite, which she fulfilled after matriculation.

In the early 1940's she was selected by the Royal Family of Belgium to tutor the Princess, a distinction which she cherished all her life.

In 1943 she received a Master of Science Degree in Psychology, an unusual field for a woman of that time. By the following year, the expectation began to grow that the terrible war was winding down to some sort of close. That same year her mother, who lived with her, died. She later completed her Ph.D. in Psychology at the University of Louvain, graduating *summa cum laude* in 1948 at the top of her otherwise all-male class.

Loving travel and the experience of the new, and without family obligations to keep her home, she came to visit her American "liberators," disembarking December 19, 1948, during a snow storm, in Hoboken, New Jersey—and wondering what (where!) in the world she had gotten herself into.

In 1949, she enrolled in a post-doctoral Counseling Program at Columbia University, and in 1950 participated in the Clinical Observation Program through New York University at Bellevue Hospital.

She had happy memories of living at International House in New York and in Chicago, where she entered the University of Chicago Clinical Psychology Program under Dr. Carl R. Rogers, a pioneer in the revolution in Psychology that was to become known as Humanistic Psychology.[7] She was fond of telling a story from her Chicago days of a *LIFE* magazine reporter who came to a lecture she gave at the clinic. Learning, there, the details of her doctoral thesis (an examination of a projective technique as a guide to personality[8]), he enthusiastically proposed doing a story in *LIFE*. Still a recently transplanted European and totally unaware of the magazine's reputation, she abruptly refused, (naively) annoyed that her serious academic efforts might be thought grist for the popular media. When her American colleagues heard this in a faculty meeting, they persuaded her to grant the interview, and the article was published.[9]

In her own words, her postdoctoral program "was undertaken for the purpose of becoming acquainted with the thinking and practice of counseling and psychotherapy in its various approaches and in its various applications (individual, child, group)."

Dr. Kinget's European education was in philosophy and Freudian psychoanalysis, there being no other psychology at that time. Her American experience introduced her to the Humanistic Psychology approach, "[focused] on the whole man, rather than on isolated data,...[dealing] with both feeling *and* fact, behavior *and* experience, unconscious *and* conscious processes, the tangible *and* the imponderable–the whole of it considered in the perspective of integration, not only of analysis."[10] From among the answers to the "important question" of the nature of man, she chose the Humanistic approach, in its scholarly reaches, as being more intellectually and experientially sound.[11]

In 1952 she joined the faculty at Michigan State University in East Lansing, Michigan, where, at the time of her death in 1997, she was Emerita Professor.

During the intervening years, she taught psychology and developed two courses which were "firsts" in the country: her board-approved "Humanistic Psychology" and "The Psychology of Love and Maturity." She co-authored several books with Carl Rogers;[12] wrote books, chapters, articles and presented papers at international meetings;[13] and maintained a private practice in psychotherapy.

In the early 1970's Harcourt Brace Jovanovich Publishers invited her to submit a manuscript dealing with Humanistic Psychology; in 1975 her *On Being Human: A Systematic View,*[14] considered a classic in the field, was published. It has been said that every book is, in some sense, autobiographical. Therefore, it is to Professor Kinget's writings, and to *On Being Human* especially, that we can turn for an intellectual and existential biography and to situate *The Master-Myth of Modern Society*.[15]

Professor Kinget's over-all aim in *On Being Human*, and, indeed, in her life's work as professor, psychotherapist, and author, is/was to make the human being known to himself–*in his full nature*–and to contribute to "the development of a psychology of the whole man." Opposing the natural science model of psychology–yielding the model of man as *solely* biological machine–she describes the attributes that distinguish man from all else: "the capacity for reflective thought, for declarative language, for devising symbols, laws, tools that make tools, wills, games, in one word: culture, in its revelation of man as the only animal who exists, knowingly, in space-time, who manifests transcendental and metaphysical concern throughout history and culture." By systematically "mapping out" the specific function and characteristics of man in *On Being Human*, she presents "the fundamentals to any valid approach to psychology," and, "at the same time, [hopes] that the approach formulates a tentative basis for the answer to the essential question that everyone must work out for himself: *What is man for?*"[16]

Consonant with the goal of enlightening modern Western man about the human condition, and with a rather more thera-peutic concern, Dr. Kinget's monograph, *Pleasure And Pain*,[17] provides "certain insights potentially capable of preventing or alleviating, in some small measure, the bitterness and destruc-tiveness that may result from a crippling ignorance about…the pleasure-pain dimension of human existence." She presents evi-dence of the largely unrecognized *interdependence* of pleasure and pain; refutes what she calls "the *disasterously wide-spread fallacy that fun lies in the means* when it actually lies in the subject"; and discusses the potential for the personal, autonomous "management" of pleasure and pain in the face of "cultural dictates [which] impede the action of self-regulating human functions."

Dr. Kinget's articles extend her attempts to heighten the level of awareness of existentially significant issues, to create conditions conducive to the enrichment of modern consciousness. In "The 'Many-Splendored Thing' In Transition Or 'The Agony And The Ecstasy' Revisited," she proposes that romantic love is "going through a radical change, not only in its observable manifestations as a behavioral phenomenon, but, substantially, as an experience...." She lists the technological and socio-political conditions responsible for the decline of romantic love–for the "elimination of certain deep feelings and intense emotions"– and discusses the potential positive and negative effects on individuals and society of "an emotional impoverishment entailing a certain flattening of personality."[18]

Written with a beauty of style that becomes part of its message, "Life From Death" brings into relief the necessity of at least a peripheral awareness of death in order for life to be lived meaningfully and effectively. Realization of the "sharp boundary" of death lends life value and necessitates "personality-shaping choices....When threads of death's rough yarn are judiciously, almost artistically woven into the fabric of existence, experience acquires 'texture'–preventing it from slipping, unawares, into nothingness."[19]

In "Psychotherapy: A Journey, Not a Destination, or Rogerian Psychotherapy Revisited," Dr. Kinget summarizes the Rogerian approach to therapy which has been described in several books by Dr.'s Rogers and/or Kinget[20]: "The first to be exclusively and thoroughly novel, both in its theory and its...typically North American approach–reflecting the ideals...of democracy, autonomy, and private enterprise"–its key concept is the affirmation of human capacity. Coupled with the basic organismal tendency toward orthogenic growth, and in a "relationship characterized by empathic understanding, unconditional regard, and authenticity... the capacity of the human being to understand his or her own self and problems [can be realized] to the extent necessary to take constructive action." The potential capacity to discover "that cluster of needs and values that constitutes the real, operational self" can be actualized "through the release of forces from within." She contrasts the Rogerian approach with the "cultural stereotype according to which, in matters of treatment, positive change can come about only through external, expert action."[21]

Among the evaluative writings at the time of psychology's centennial, the great majority decrying the fact that "objective psychology...particularly in its theoretical-behavioral sector... [had] failed to mature into a coherent, valid discipline," Dr. Kinget contributed "Objective Psychology: A Case of Epistomological Sleight-Of-Hand." In reviewing the history of the development of psychology, its choice of method and its theoretical premises, she concludes that:

> It is increasingly apparent that the infirmity is congenital–psychology having been planted in alien soil, without even the beginnings of an authentic epistomological root-system. [In choosing the physical model of scientific investigation, few of the early psychologists] apparently ever stopped to ask the crucial epistomological question, to wit: whether the phenomena of consciousness, though doubtlessly natural, are natural *in the same sense* as the phenomena studied by the natural sciences.
>
> This epistomological neglect and the resulting methodological error...introduced an ideology under the cloak of methodology–the mechanistic, Newtonian ideology which dominated 19th century thinking. The central assumption of this crypto-ideological methodology is the belief that psychological phenomena can be

studied in the same way as physico-chemical phenomena...[implying] that...they are identical in their nature....This amounts to a leveling of phenomena that clearly belong to different cognitive strata ...ignoring...precisely what constitutes the specificity or identity of the phenomenon (it should be noted that even physics...respects phenomenal differences, e.g., different approaches are devised for dealing with mechanics, fluids, electricity)....What the researcher owes allegiance to, first and foremost, is the integrity of the phenomena–not his necessarily tentative and possibly erroneous methodology.

Closely related to the preceding is objective psychology's firmly established practice of equating the unique case of human experience with the single case of physical research... substituting quantity for specificity...and [shifting the use of] the term "fact" from physics [where it is understood as that which can be replicated and verified by other observers] to consciousness...[where] there is not necessarily a demonstrable correspondence between the life-world of the subject's response and the experimenter's logical operations about this response....

Objective psychology also...manages to ignore the absolutely peculiar, oft-mentioned, seldom heeded fact of the identical nature of the subject and experimenter in human research–a peculiarity which clamors for an epistomological substructure *sui generis*....

Finally, under the guise of dealing with humans *qua* organisms pure and simple, objective psychology deals with irretrievably encultured systems which tolerate no separation of culture and biology. [22]

The *specifically human* characteristics, the focus (explicitly or implicitly) of all of Professor Kinget's works, derive from man's unique symbolic capacity,

the purest and most complex manifestation of which is conceptual thought....The capacity for conceptual thought, [being independent of the immediate sensory stimulation required for the perceptual thinking typical of animals], enables man to think in terms of...the future, not yet given...[allowing] him to conceive of alternate courses of action and to compare them in terms of logical, practical, or moral principles. Thus, conceptual thought provides the basic, systemic condition for human freedom.[23]

A lifetime labor (and love) of logical explication, illustration and dissemination of a view of the human being in all of his fullness, complexity, and freedom, presupposed a co-existent alternate, at best incomplete, model of man. In "Objective Psychology: A Case of Epistomological Sleight-Of-Hand," Dr. Kinget has specifically elucidated the most fundamental of academic psychology's epistomological errors—resulting in and from the adoption of the physical science model for studying the human being. This methodological model, long outdated *in the physical sciences* at the time of her writings, produced that alternate model of man, the "diminished and fragmented image"[24] of the human being determined *entirely* by genes and environment.

The choice and retention of the natural science model for studying man—and acceptance of the image of man that it projects—derive from the all-encompassing scientific worldview of modern society. It is this scientific worldview, "not the scientific enterprise itself but...the rhetoric, the ideology, indeed, the mystique which surrounds science and its achievements," which Dr. Kinget characterizes and critically evaluates as the "master-myth" in the present work—*myth* understood as a perennial psycho-social phenomenon, "expressing an internal compulsion toward making sense out of the vast unknown...an urge to understand in a comprehensive way."

She begins by defining *myth*, its origins, and function as a living reality for the individual and society. She tests the scientific worldview for its "fit" within that definition, and evaluates it according to the beneficial or debilitating qualities of its effects. She presents as an essential element within the myth of the scientific worldview, the concept of *objective* knowledge, and characterizes the firm hold on modern man of the idea of *objectivity* as "a way of being." Through common sense analysis of "science-in-the-making" and pointing to confirmatory findings in the field of quantum physics, she explains that "there is no such thing as objectivity," and casts that notion, too, in the context of living myth.

Commenting that man's questions and answers are in the process of being reconstructed, noting modern man's "over-riding appetite for psychological insight," and referring to Jung's view of that "appetite" as a reflection of a spiritual need, Professor Kinget concludes with a development of what may be the "promise of Psychology" for modern man and his society.

I write this Foreword as one of those Americans Professor Kinget describes as having been schooled in systems, inaugurated after World War II, preparing individuals for success in our scientific and technological society—but treating sparingly of "an introduction to man's nature, his history and destiny."

The main criticism received during my inquiries concerning the posthumous publication of this particular work of Dr. Kinget's centered around its time-specificity, written as it was over twenty years ago. My response is this: It is the members of my generation who are, as Librarian of Congress Billington highlights, currently neglecting the "important questions." And it is my generation, as parents and teachers of the next, who will pass on this legacy of avoiding, or failing even to recognize, the humanly essential issues. With the new frontiers of science being the molecular and the mind, the questions of the nature of the human being, and of the appropriate methodologies to be used in the search for answers, loom at least as large as when Dr. Kinget was writing. Then, the revolution in quantum physics transformed the philosophical theory of perception, so that the theme of the subjective, human element in *all* knowledge now predominates in epistomology. But has its significance been established concretely in other, specialized disciplines, and has it been assimilated by the layman?

The question of man's nature is "so large and multifaceted that it does not yield to the modern sesame of specialization."[25] It is a "mixed question, [one] that cannot be adequately answered by scientists alone or by philosophers alone, but only...by combining the findings of scientific investigation with the contributions of philosophical analysis and criticism";[26] "scientific formulations are merely descriptive, philosophical knowledge is explanatory."[27] It is the generalist with a certain sensibility, clarity of insight, and genius for synthesis who contributes most significantly to the enlargement of humanly meaningful knowledge.

"Ideas about man have the most far-reaching consequences of all. Upon them may depend the structure of government, the patterns of culture, the purposes of education, the design of the future—and the human or inhuman [treatment] of human beings."[28] We are a global community, with our humanness as our singular commonality. As we take stock of our century, we are still in need, more than ever, it seems, of Dr. Adler's "Summa Dialectica." Works such as Professor Kinget's are at the existential center of that desired "common medium of exchange for all mankind"; they are at the heart of that ideal "single universe of discourse"; they serve as example of an answer to the call for intellectual expansion—still being sounded—transcending the limitations of the specialist point of view. Within the context of revitalizing the intellectual enterprise, they assume a permanent importance.

— *With gratitude for the example of a life lived with a focused awareness of ultimate questions.*

A.A.W. 1999

NOTES TO THE FOREWORD

1. Adler, Mortimer J. "The Philosopher." In *The Works of the Mind*, edited by Robert B. Heywood. Chicago, Illinois: University of Chicago Press, 1947, pp. 245-246.
2. Morrison, M. "Marian Kinget: A Gentle Rebel." *MSU Faculty Bulletin*, Nov. 20, 1975, p. 4.
3. Kinget, G. Marian. *On Being Human and Pleasure and Pain: Two Humanistic Works*. Lanham, Maryland: University Press of America, 1999, p. xxiv.
4. Tolson, Jay. "A Meeting of the Minds, With a Nod To Yesterday." *U.S. News & World Report*, June 28, 1999, p. 61.
5. Billington, James H. Quoted by Tolson. *Ibid.*
6. Adler, Mortimer J. "Man." In *The Great Ideas: A Lexicon of Western Thought*. New York: Macmillan Publishing Company, 1992, p. 462.
7. Inside the cover of a 1962 edition of *Psychothérapie et Relations Humaines, Théorie et Pratique de la Thérapie Non-Directive*, Vol. I, Exposé Général (Part I authored in French by G. M. Kinget; Part II authored by Carl R. Rogers, translated into French by G. M. Kinget), a hand-written note of Dr. Kinget's was found which reads: "To the best of my knowledge the term *humanistic* was first used in Psychology in the book I wrote with Rogers [she then gives the title above]...Vol. I, p. 103." See Note 12 below for the complete citation for this book.
8. Kinget, G. Marian. *The Drawing-Completion Test. A Projective Technique for the Investigation of Personality Based on the Wartegg Test Blank*. New York: Grune and Stratton, 1964 (2nd ed.)
9. Luce, Henry R., ed. "Complete These Drawings," *LIFE*, June 9, 1952, pp. 65-68.
10. Kinget, G. Marian. *On Being Human and Pleasure and Pain: Two Humanistic Works*, p. xx.
11. "Once the psychoanalytic monopoly was broken, the doors for psychotherapeutic initiative were flung wide open....Modification and expansion between the two leading and *virtually antithetical* systems...basically were offshoots...from these fountainheads, enriched by bridging efforts and sometimes brilliant insights." (Kinget, G. Marian. "Psychotherapy: A Journey, Not a Destination, or Rogerian Psychotherapy Revisited." In: *International Psychotherapy: Theories, Research, and Cross-Cultural Implications*. L. Simek-Morgan, ed. Westport, CT: Greenwood Press, Inc., 1989, pp. 97-98.)

12. Books co-authored with Carl Rogers include the following:

Rogers, Carl R. and G. Marian Kinget. *Psychotherapie en Menselijke Verhoudingen, Theorie en Praktijk van de Non-Directieve Therapie.* Utrecht, Nederlands: Uitgeverij Het Spectrum, 1959. Paperback, Den Haag, Nederlands: Uitgeverij Bert Bakker, 1974. (Part I authored, in Dutch, by G. M. Kinget; Part II authored by Carl Rogers, translated into Dutch by G. M. Kinget.)

Rogers, Carl R. and G. Marian Kinget. *Psychothérapie et Relations Humaines, Théorie et Pratique de la Thérapie Non-Directive.* Vol. I, Exposé Général. In: Studia Psychologica, Sous La Direction De A. Michotte et J. Nuttin. Louvain, Belgium: Publications Universitaires De Louvain; Paris, France: Editions Beatrice-Nauwelaerts, 1962. Seventh edition, 1976. (Part I authored in French by G. M. Kinget; Part II authored by Carl Rogers, translated into French by G. M. Kinget.)

Rogers, Carl R. and G. Marian Kinget. *Psychothérapie et Relations Humaines, Théorie et Pratique de la Thérapie Non-Directive.* Vol. II, La Pratique par G. Marian Kinget. In: Studia Psychologica, Sous La Direction De A. Michotte et J. Nuttin. Louvain, Belgium: Publications Universitaires De Louvain; Paris, France: Editions Beatrice-Nauwelaerts, 1962. Seventh edition, 1976. (Entirely authored in French by G .M. Kinget.)

Rogers, Carl y G. Marian Kinget. *Psicoterapia y Relaciones Humanas, Teoria y Practica De La Terapia No Directiva.* Tomo I. Exposición General. In: Hombres, Hechos e Ideas, XIV. Madrid, Spain: Ediciones Alfaguara, 1967. (Part I authored by G. M. Kinget; Part II authored by Carl Rogers; translated into Spanish by Mercedes Valcarce.)

Rogers, Carl y G. Marian Kinget. *Psicoterapia y Relaciones Humanas, Teoria y Practica De La Terapia No Dirigida.* Tomo II. La Práctica por G. Marian Kinget. In: Hombres, Hechos e Ideas, XIV. Orense, Spain: Ediciones Alfaguara, 1967. (Entirely authored by G. M. Kinget; translated into Spanish by Mercedes Valcarce.)

Rogers, Carl R. e G. Marian Kinget. *Psicoterapia e Ralazioni Umane, Teoria e Prática Della Terapia Non Direttiva.* Testi e manuali della scienza contemporanea, Serie di psicologia e psichiatria. Torino, Italy: Boringhieri, 1970. (Part I authored by G. M. Kinget; Part II authored by C. Rogers; Part III authored by G. M. Kinget; translated into Italian by Rosetta Galli.)

Rogers, Carl R. e G. Marian Kinget. *Psicoterapia e Relações Humanas, Teoria e Prática da Terapia Não-Diretiva.* Vol. I, Exposição Geral. Belo Horizonte, Brazil: Interlivros, 1975. (Part I authored by G. M. Kinget; Part II authored by Carl Rogers; translated into Portuguese by Maria Luisa Bizzotta.)

Rogers, Carl R. e G. Marian Kinget. *Psicoterapia e Relações Humanas, Teoria e Prática da Terapia Não-Diretiva.* Vol. II, Exposição Geral. Belo Horizonte, Brazil: Interlivros, 1975. (Entirely authored by G. M. Kinget; translated into Portuguese by Maria Luisa Bizzotta.)

13. Individual scholarly works include:

Kinget, G. Marian. *Intuitieve Psychologie vs. Experimentele Psychologie.* In: Miscell. Jubil., J. Gessler, ed. Louvain, Belgium: Universitaire Pers., 1949.

Kinget. *The Drawing Completion Test.* 1952, 1964.

Kinget, G. Marian. "Personality Assessment." *International House Quarterly.* Spring 1953, pp. 69-76.

Kinget, G. Marian. "The Drawing Completion Test." In: *The Clinical Application of Projective Drawings,* F. G. Hammer, ed. Springfield, Illinois: Charles E. Thomas, 1958, pp. 344-364.

Kinget, G. Marian. *On Being Human: A Systematic View.* New York: Harcourt Brace Jovanovich, Inc., 1975. (Second edition: Lanham, Maryland: University Press of America, 1987).

Kinget, G. Marian. *Lun Jen.* (*On Being Human*) Translated into Chinese by Nai-ch'en Ch'en. T'ai-pei: Ch'eng Wen Ch'u Pan She, 1978.

Kinget, G. Marian. "Life From Death." *Dawnpoint, A Journal of the Association for Humanistic Psychology.* Vol. I, No. 2, pp. 40-44, 1978.

Kinget, G. Marian. "The 'Many-Splendored Thing' in Transition or 'The Agony and the Ecstasy' Revisited." In: *Love and Attraction: An International Conference.* M. Cook and G. Wilson, eds. New York: Pergamon Press, 1978, pp. 251-254.

Kinget. "Psychotherapy: A Journey, Not a Destination, or Rogerian Therapy Revisited."

Kinget, G. Marian. "Objective Psychology: A Case of Epistomological Sleight-of-Hand." Journal of Phenomenological Psychology, Vol. II, No. 1, pp. 83-96, 1990.

Kinget, G. Marian. "Variations dans la Perception du Moi en Fonction de Variations dans le Niveau d'Anxiete." Presented at the 15th International Congress of Psychology, Brussels, Belgium, 1957.

Kinget, G. Marian. "The 'Many-Splendored Thing' in Transition or 'The Agony and the Ectasy' Revisited." Presented at Love and Attraction: An International Conference, University College of Swansea, Wales, September 5-9, 1977.

Kinget, G. Marian. "Psychology as an Awakening of Personal Competence and Emotional Maturity or Rogerian Psychotherapy Revisited." Presented at the International Conference on Psychotherapy, Bogota, Columbia, February 24-27, 1983.

14. *On Being Human* is currently available in its third edition: see Note 3 above.

15. *The Master-Myth of Modern Society* was originally a lecture and the last of the unpublished works found posthumously in draft form among Dr. Kinget's papers, though not chronologically the last of her writings:

Kinget. "Life From Death." 1978.

Kinget. "The 'Many-Splendored Thing' in Transition or 'The Agony and the Ecstasy' Revisited." 1978.

Kinget. "Psychotherapy: A Journey, Not a Destination, or Rogerian Psychotherapy Revisited." 1989.

Kinget. "Objective Psychology: A Case of Epistomological Sleight-of-Hand." 1990.

16. Kinget. *On Being Human and Pleasure and Pain*, pp. xxviii, 2, 176.

17. *Pleasure and Pain* is available for the first time in the 1999 combined volume: see Note 3 above.

18. Kinget. "The 'Many-Splendored Thing' in Transition or 'The Agony and the Ecstasy' Revisited," pp. 251, 253.

19. Kinget. "Life From Death," pp. 42-43.

20. In addition to those listed in Note 12 above, see the following:

Rogers, Carl R. and Leonard Carmichael. *Counseling and Psychotherapy: Newer Concepts in Practice.* Boston: Houghton Mifflin Company, 1942.

Rogers, Carl R. *Client-Centered Therapy: Its Practice, Implications, and Theory.* Boston: Houghton Mifflin Company, 1951.

Rogers, Carl R. *On becoming A Person: A Therapist's View of Psychotherapy.* Boston: Houghton Mifflin Company, 1961; 1995.

Rogers, Carl R. *A Way Of Being.* Boston: Houghton Mifflin Company, 1980; 1995.

Kinget. *On Being Human.* 1975; 1987.

Kinget. *On Being Human and Pleasure and Pain.* 1999.

21. Kinget. "Psychotherapy: A Journey, Not a Destination, or Rogerian Psychotherapy Revisited," pp. 98, 101, 102, 105.

22. Kinget. "Objective Psychology: A Case of Epistomological Sleight-of-Hand," pp. 83, 84, 86-90.
23. Kinget. *On Being Human and Pleasure and Pain*, pp. 23, 30.
24. *Ibid.*, p. 241.
25. Noonan, John T. "The Measurement of Morals." Paper presented at the symposium, "Frontiers of the Mind in the 21st Century." Washington, D.C.: Library of Congress, June, 1999.
26. Adler, Mortimer J. *The Difference of Man and the Difference It Makes.* New York: Holt, Rinehart and Winston, 1967, p. 13.
27. Adler, Mortimer J. "The Philosopher," p. 226.
28. Matson, Floyd W. *The Idea Of Man.* New York: Delacorte Press, 1976, pp. 11-12.

ACKNOWLEDGMENTS

For permission to use the selections reprinted in this book, the author is grateful to the following publishers and copyright holders:

Bobbs-Merrill Company, Inc. For excerpts from *A Civil Tongue* by Edwin Newman. Copyright 1975, 1976 by Edwin H. Newman. Reprinted by permission of the author.

Gerald A. Larue. For excerpts from *Ancient Myth and Modern Man*. Copyright 1975 by Gerald A. Larue. Reprinted by permission of the author.

Simon and Schuster Trade, Inc. For an excerpt from *The Decline of Pleasure* by Walter Kerr. Copyright 1962 by Walter Kerr. Reprinted by permission of Jean Kerr.

INTRODUCTION

For several years the Michigan State University department of humanities has been offering the interdisciplinary, capstone course, Humanities 499, "Great Issues," devoted to the "analysis and discussion of selected problems challenging the modern world," and "centering on such issues as the impact of science and technology on society, war and peace, civil liberties, race relations, and self-identity in mass society." (Krupka, 1976) Since such issues often have psychological dimensions, psychologists are apt to be part of the teaching team.

When asked to participate, I was puzzled to learn that the topic for Spring 1977 was *myth*. Inflation being rampant in academia as elsewhere, I wondered: Are fanciful tales now regarded as "Great Issues"? Hardly inclined toward a topic which, in times contending with truly great issues, seemed almost shockingly trivial, and aware of my limited competence in matters of myth, I was tempted to decline the offer. But my belief in the excellence of the organizers' judgment nudged me to see whether, *per impossible,* some helpful hints for modern man's predicament might arise from stories about that mixed lot of gods, demi-gods, and chosen earthlings which typically form the cast of myths, East and West.

The hunch paid off: Research soon revealed a large wedge of scholarship of whose existence–rather, of whose precise focus and level of development–I had been only faintly aware. In the process, some incipient thoughts I had long been harboring on the subject were stirred into awareness, causing my motivation to rise by several notches.

1. Myth as Story and Myth as Fact

Myth, I thus discovered, had been the object of systematic and expanding investigation since around the middle of the 19th century, when a number of researchers from a variety of fields successively began to examine myth as a potential source of valuable data and insights. Leading the way was philology (Müller, 1897), followed by anthropology (Lang, 1897; Tylor, 1920; Malinowski, 1936, 1948, also, Strenski, ed., 1992), psychoanalysis (Jung, 1933), sociology (Durkheim, 1915), religion (Gunkel, translated 1964), history (Eliade, 1949), and of recent date, psychology (Murray, 1960). In the process of expanding, the study of myth differentiated. New foci emerged, consequently new approaches developed, eventuating in the creation of new fields. Traditionally the study of myth focused exclusively upon content and exclusively ancient content. Today it has two foci, one dealing with content–either secular or ancient; the other centering upon the fact of myth as a psycho-social phenomenon exhibiting a remarkable constancy in nature and function throughout space and time.

2. The Empirical vs. The Literary Approach to Myth

Methodologically, this shift *from fiction to fact* and *from ancient to modern*, corresponds to a change *from narrative reporting to observation and hypothesizing* with a view toward explanation. The traditional, purely descriptive approach, focused upon content, is still called mythology or literature of myth and remains a province of classics. The new empirical approach or, as some authors actually call it (a bit prematurely), "the science of myth" (Jung and Kerenyi, 1963), falls within the broad compass of the social sciences. For this new concept of myth reveals itself as a source of promising material for the study of man and culture–of man as a system of built-in universal needs and tendencies; of culture as the whole of the conditions in which those needs and tendencies express themselves in time and space.

According to a different classification, this new approach to myth falls within the incipient field of meta-psychology. The present paper deals with issues forming, as it were, the interface of these two disciplines, social science and meta-psychology.

PART ONE

Nature and Function of Myth

1. What Myth is Not

Because the word *myth* now has two meanings, one referring to a thing of imagination, the other to an observable phenomenon, the empirical approach to myth, fertile though it is, poses a problem for all but the specialist. Myth in the traditional sense of legend or fallacy is so firmly entrenched in current usage that the new technical meaning has trouble gaining currency, indeed, merely getting to be known—not only by the general public but within the educated community as well.

Therefore, it seems essential to begin by stressing what myth in the new context does *not* signify: *myth should not be lumped in one category with the notions of legend, fable, folklore, and related creations of human imagination.* More strongly: myth should not be equated with plain falsehood or fallacy, as commonly occurs, for example, in Thomas Szasz' well-known *The Myth of Mental Illness* (1974) in which he denies all validity to the concept of "mental" illness. The differentiation now made between myth and fanciful tales (that used to be regarded as germane) does not mean, however, that their categories are always clearly delineated, especially where ancient myths are concerned. Myth and tale do maintain a phenotypical or surface resemblance. For myth is a complex, paradoxical notion, as will become apparent.

Another distinction needs emphasis from the outset: Myth and myth-making are not confined either to the distant past or to preliterate cultures. Being an expression of an inherently human need, myth-making is an ongoing, spontaneously unfolding psycho-social process, found always and everywhere. Only themes and style vary with time and culture.

Also, myth is not some individual creation or persuasion but a pervasively *collective, cognitive-emotional* representation. Only those beliefs having currency within a culture or subculture, only those honored and sanctioned by the group, qualify as myths. Private, emotionalized beliefs, no matter how encompassing or fervently held, are either idiosyncrasies, illusions, or delusions.

Particularly important to dispel is the notion that myths necessarily deal with gods, supernatural beings, or heroes–though most ancient myths feature these. If such were the case, there would be no secular myths, when actually most current myths are secular in content. However–and this hints at the complexity (though also the fascination) of myth–while they may be purely secular in theme and origin, myths concern issues so fundamental, offer answers so "unassailable" that they partake of the absoluteness associated with things religious. Therefore, as Eliade notes, myths can be regarded as "sacral in an extended sense."

Finally, myth is not a form of entertainment addressed to fanciful imagination. Rather, it reflects a worldview–with all the seriousness that notion conveys. One clear way to distinguish myth from folk-tale and legend is precisely, as Malinowski (1948, pp. 72-124) emphasizes, *the weight of its significance* for establishing criteria of truth and reality, for confirming rights and institutions, and for reflecting persistent psycho-social problems and preoccupations.

In sum, myth and mythmaking are not optional, frivolous, or private projections. Neither are they confined to particular cultures or particular historical periods. On the contrary. They represent compelling, irrepressible manifestations of the human psyche, confronted by the vast questions arising from the experience of self and the world.

2. The Essence of Myth

Where complex notions are concerned, especially those surrounded by lingering ambiguity, it is far easier to say what something is *not* than to say what it actually is. The following suggests some of the paradoxes inherent in the concept of myth.

A first, skeleton-like definition of the concept of myth in its new empirical meaning can be gained from simply transposing into positive terms the negative characteristics stated in the preceding section. Thus, myth appears as 1) expressing truth rather than fallacy; 2) a modern phenomenon, as well as an ancient one; 3) collective rather than individual in origin and nature; 4) dealing with people of any kind rather than exclusively with supernatural or heroic figures. But this definition, though legitimate, fails to convey the living reality of myth–as distinct from its archival counterpart, whether ancient or modern.

"A Lie That is True" or "The Only Valid Revelation of Reality"?

The difficulty in characterizing the essence of myth lies mainly with the assertion that myth is true–which it is, though only in a peculiar sense. Donald Stauffer in "The Modern Myth of the Modern Myth" feels that LaFontaine's clever and self-reflecting epigram, "A fable is a lie that tells the truth," conveys the essence of myth. Actually, just the opposite seems applicable: Myth is a truth covering a lie–and Stauffer's own commentary seems to be addressed to the latter rather than to the former characterization:

> The myth, as I conceive it, tends toward a lie at least to the extent that it is not verifiable in science or history. And it tells the truth to the extent that people *believe* that it tells the truth....The myth helps them in their beliefs. It satisfies a desire or a need. It answers a riddle. (Stauffer, in Wimsatt, 1974, p. 66)

Less paradoxically phrased, myth is true phenomenologically from the point of view of the group that incarnates the myth. But ontologically, from the (purely theoretical) point of view of the "truly true," the "really real," myth is bound to be partially, even totally erroneous–at the very least, unverifiable. Stated in yet another way: As psycho-social phenomenon, myth is real. But its contents, themes, and accounts are speculative in the uniquely unintentional, largely unconscious, diffusely emotionalized way typical of projections. For myths are projections (in the non-psychoanalytical sense of this word), collective mental projections providing symbolic answers to the common questions and concerns of mankind–concerns related to origins (How did it all start?), identity (Who am I?), conduct and goals (What is right? What is happiness?), eschatology (After this, what?). In sum, myth represents man's intuitive-imaginative defense against his ignorance about the nature of what he experiences within and around him. It aims to explain "why the world is as it is," (Larue, 1975, p. 6) and is experienced as obviously and unquestionably true or, as Eliade puts it, "the only valid revelation of reality." (1957, p. 24)

Myth Must Live Incognito

Essential to the nature and power of myth is that the community *not* realize that it *is* myth. That is, fiction—or mixture of fact and fiction. Collective beliefs and emotions fully recognized as myth lose their power to influence, e.g., the myths about the denizens of Mt. Olympus in ancient Greece or the myth of the frontier in America. It is the myth we accept without question that holds sway over us. Living myth is unrecognized myth, and just as archaic society accepted it unconditionally, so does modern man—as long as it is not effectively punctured.

Myth is of All Times

All authorities on the subject insist that myth is not only something of the ancient past. Myth is perennial. More unbelievable yet, indeed, almost mortifying, is the experts' unanimous assertion that just as archaic man experienced the mythic explanation of his time as obviously and unquestionably true—so does modern man.* Even the basic structure of the contents of myth reveals a distinct similarity throughout history and cultures—though themes may vary widely as a comparison between ancient and modern (especially contemporary) myth reveals.

The perennial character of myth is rooted in the fact that man, as the symbolic animal, reflects on his observations and experience. He alone in the universe ponders his existence and his world. This reflective capacity, this urge to understand, combines with his eminently social nature which inclines him

---

*In a humorous (though nowise preposterous) vein, one can recognize the pattern of myth and cult in the very operation of the scientific community. Who would argue that the researchers' hypotheses and theories—however fruitful many of them—are literally leading fictions; that professors are major myth-mediators; that exams have much in common with initiation rites; that certain areas of thought and even certain words are taboo; that com-

toward taking consensus for truth. The collective representations thus generated crystallize the central values and mental-emotional commitment of a given culture (Roszak, 1969). Myth, then, forms an indispensable ingredient of culture at all times.

Stamped by the Group

The *collective* character of myth may already be clear enough to warrant brief treatment. Suffice it to compare that characteristic to the notion of *Zeitgeist* (literally: spirit of the age) as the sum of the dominant psychic, spiritual, and social impressions that stamp an individual as belonging either to classical antiquity, medieval Christianity, the romantic or the modern era. Like *Zeitgeist*, myth possesses an enduring, pervasive power to influence and mold from which the particular individual can hardly escape—situated, as he is, in a particular cultural and historical context—and from which, moreover, he hardly wishes to escape. For while myth is confining, it is *shared* confinement and represents, therefore, a haven of security.

Secular Yet "Absolute"

Two other, related characteristics of myth deserve amplification in modern context. First, in contrast with its ancient model, modern myth does not necessarily (if at all) deal with heroes or otherwise superhuman characters but focuses upon everyman, the masses and the impersonal forces that shape and move mankind. Second, myth is not necessarily concerned with religion, especially organized religion. Yet, like all mythic representations, modern secular myth can be considered religious

---

mencements and annual conventions partake of ancient ritual festivals, with the celebration of feats of intellectual prowess and the awarding of honors to the "heroes," all this together with symposia—in the original sense of convivial meetings usually followed by a dinner, for drinking, conversation, and intellectual entertainment.

in a metaphoric sense, as suggested in the following passage by Eliade:

> among the "primitives" as among the moderns, the sacred is manifested in a multitude of forms and variants, but...all these hierophanies are charged with *power*. The sacred is strong, powerful, because it is *real*; it is efficacious and durable. The opposition between sacred and profane is often expressed as an opposition between the *real* and the *unreal* or pseudo-real.... One must not, of course, expect to find in the archaic language the pretentious terminology of the philosophers: *Real-Unreal*, etc. – but we do encounter *the thing*. For the consciousness of the archaic peoples, the *strong*, the *sacred*, is an expression of the *supremely real*. (1957, p. 130)

Because of these intimations of strength, power, and reality, myths, like religions, tend to affect man as "statements about the absolute." In Kerenyi's formulation:

> I have here used the word 'absolute' as a description, as non-committal as possible, for everything before which a man stands *religiously*, as before the divine. We have here the original sense of the word 'religious', not referring to a particular religion, but to an attitude of respect, or beyond that, of worship, or more still, a feeling of giddiness on the edge of the abyss, of the Nihil, or 'nothingness'. (1962, p. 14)

Incidentally, this "attitude of respect," indeed, of reverence brings to mind the fascination and awe experienced by modern man confronted by some of the achievements of the Atomic Age, such as the space launchings at Cape Kennedy. Similar feelings were dramatically (if unintentionally) reflected in both the verbal and physiognomic language of some of the physicists featured on the television program, *Nova*, dealing with quarks and linear accelerators.

In conclusion, because of the weight and mystery of the issues to which they lend meaning, and because of the collective involvement of the community, myth tends to partake of the realm of the transcendent. As Schelling long ago recognized, "in profundity, permanence and universality, myth is comparable only with nature herself." (Schelling, 1857, in Jung and Kerenyi, 1963, p.1; 155)

3. Life Affirming vs. Debilitating Myths

With respect to the role they play within the human community, some myths are fertile, beneficial, genuinely strengthening and supportive, serving an adaptive, integrative, evolutionary role. Others tend to be vicarious, debilitating, sterile, even destructive. The former could be called authentic–performing their life-affirming function; the latter, inauthentic–failing to perform that function, even counteracting it.

More precisely, authentic myths lend meaning to the chaos of experience; they make sense of things–not only intellectually but existentially. They satisfy man's need for a feeling of purpose and worth, by sustaining his belief in, for example, the reality of progress, the possibility of justice, the value of love. Within the self they tend to promote a state of harmony, peace of mind, self-enhancement, and stability. With respect to the universe (more precisely, the topocosm, that part of the universe of which man is aware and in actual contact), authentic myth fosters an attitude of reverence, of acknowledged interdependency and responsibility reminiscent of the kind of relationship which archaic man entertained with his surroundings. Nature, to him, was personified or animated–populated and regulated by gods whom he revered and with whom he endeavored to entertain mutually satisfactory relations. In Larue's words:

> In ancient times…the world was infected with personality. The
> soil, the seed, and the crops were all part of the topocosm in which
> man lived–a world composed not of self and external things, but
> of personalities and divine beings…. All life was seen in terms of
> relationships. (1975, p. 10)

In contemporary secular terms, this attitude corresponds to
Buber's "I-Thou" relationship which expresses man's sense of
kinship with his fellowmen and ecosystem, and his participation
in their fate (Buber, 1970).

Inauthentic myths, by contrast, tend to be more elementary
in the sense that they cater to more primitive impulses, toward
possession, control, retribution, exploitation. Correlatively, their
demands upon man tend to be less exacting and less restraining
than those of the authentic type. This kind of myth is apt to
eventuate in feelings of isolation, guilt or estrangement–states
of mind which in turn spawn apathy, irresponsibility, anomie.
When alienated, man's relationship with others and nature tends
to be manipulative and exploitive, even his attitude toward
himself acquires an I-It orientation, e.g., the drug addict's manner
of getting his "highs" by injecting himself with the "stuff of
pleasure" instead of attempting to lift himself by his own efforts.
The same I-It relationship prevails between alienated man and
nature–which he exploits to the point of exhaustion and
destruction. Consequently, instead of heightening the meaning
of existence, of promoting survival and enhancement,
inauthentic myths tend to exert a debilitating, disintegrative
effect on both the individual and society, undermining values,
ideals, and human progress, impairing and, in certain cases,
destroying life. In a pervasively diffuse manner, the inauthentic
myth has a "de-sacralizing" effect, not necessarily in a religious
sense but in the broader sense of reducing, downgrading,
trivializing what mankind has always recognized as having worth
and dignity.

Authentic and inauthentic myths exist now as they did in the past. An example from antiquity is found in the myth of retribution and vengeance in Aeschylus' *Oresteia*; in the present it can be seen as imbedded in the radical behaviorist's assertion that man is determined completely by bio-sociological forces, and is devoid of what is commonly referred to as freedom and dignity. As myths proliferate, which they currently do, they necessarily follow inflationary trends. The current, centralized modes of information and communication that shape collective beliefs are unprecedented in the reach and power of their operation. Thus, while modern man has almost limitless opportunity for enlightenment and discovery, he is also exposed, as never before, to being divested of those beliefs and values that functioned as the guiding and nurturing forces of his existence.

4. Can Man Live Without Myths?

Biologically, there is little doubt that he can. But the biological and psychological, though distinct, are inseparable and interdependent—as advances in both fields increasingly reveal. Symbolically, however, that is, for man as a person, mythmaking appears as part of a survival system. Support for this position accrues from the fact that all known cultures have their store of myths, exhibiting patterns shared by communities widely separated in time and space. There is no evidence mankind ever lived without myth.

Mythmaking is not merely something man likes or chooses to engage in. It is the expression of an internal compulsion toward making sense out of the vast unknown. Mythmaking is as fundamental to his cognitive functioning as the use of the *a priori* categories, time, space, quantity, quality, etc. that, according to Kant, organize experience. It serves to bring unity and cogency within experience, to make it assimilable or suitable for sustaining and regulating existence. As Mark Schorer characterizes this function:

> Myths are the instruments by which we continually struggle to make our experience intelligible to ourselves. A myth is a large, controlling image that gives philosophical meaning to the facts of ordinary life; that is, which has organizing value for experience.... Without such images, experience is chaotic, fragmentary and merely phenomenal. It is the chaos of experience that creates them, and they are intended to rectify it. (Schorer, in Murray, 1960, p. 355)

Mythmaking arises, then, from an urge to understand in a comprehensive way. Understanding can be achieved in two ways: via explanation and via interpretation. *Explanation* consists of a strictly intellectual process that lends insight into the causes—genetic, historical, or constitutive—of things and events so as to make them rationally cogent and/or empirically verifiable. Explanation satisfies the demands of reason but not necessarily the need for meaning—at least not where existential, humanly relevant questions are concerned. For instance, the question "What is man?" can legitimately be answered in terms of DNA, cytogenetics, neurology, etc., but such explanations do not satisfy the profound questioning which arises from the experience of *being* human.* Therefore, as Kerenyi emphasizes, the understanding which proceeds from myth is not of the nature of an explanation put forward to satisfy scientific curiosity; it is

---

*Another example of explanation's failure to yield meaning is found in Behaviorism's radically reductionistic theories. The clarity and (mechanistic) simplicity of its explanations exert a very real appeal to the intellect (even though they are unverifiable except for elementary forms of human behavior). But the concept of the individual as a product of contingencies

the re-arising of a primordial reality–a very different form of insight (Jung and Kerenyi, 1963, pp. 7-8).

Interpretation, by contrast, lacks the precision and verifiability of explanation but goes beyond explanation in scope and depth. While it does not meet the causal criteria of the intellect, it satisfies the demands of intuition, affect, and imagination–which Jung describes as the unconscious urge to understand. Myth yields insight without straining the intellect, largely because it accounts for things not in terms of causes but of reasons. Granted, interpretation does not provide answers to specific questions. For myth pertains essentially to those vast questions, life and death, origins and destiny, for all of which that particular kind of cognitive satisfaction that Gestalt psychology calls "closure" is better suited. Also, interpretation provides more durable answers than those offered by explanation. This is part of the strength–if also the liability–of myth. For while myth is capable of generating feelings of stability and security, it is also apt to offer blind resistance to progress and enlightenment.

In summary, existentialism's tenet, "Reason alone cannot account for man," clearly applies here. Myth, as meaning, addresses itself to man as subject, not as object; and to his total being rather than solely to his intellect. Personal experience is drawn into the process and serves as criterion for the validation of the mythic account. For accounts that fail to square with experience, however valid they may be by external criteria,

---

of the situation, does not square with experience. In fact, such explanations go directly against the universal experience of free agency. Some theoreticians will explain this discrepancy by what they regard as "man's systematic tendency toward self-aggrandizement." This argument, however, can be countered by pointing to Behaviorism's systematic tendency to debunk the human being, reducing him to its "nothing but" category. Moreover, this presumed "tendency toward self-aggrandizement," if it is systematic, calls itself for explanation.

generate frustration and alienation. Psychology has shown the results of such states upon the individual and upon society.

Therapeutic Function of Myth

Because it organizes experience and generates meaning, living myth has incomparable therapeutic value in times of cultural or personal crisis (May, 1961, especially Chapter 12). The early psychoanalysts were prompt to recognize its explanatory and therapeutic potential. Closer to us, Viktor Frankl's logotherapy (Frankl, 1969) is keyed precisely to this meaning-generating function. Not only psychotherapists but even scholars of myth lacking any kind of clinical formation (Schorer, Eliade, Larue) recognize that for many, myth is integral in sustaining social and individual psychological health. For myths echo human hopes and dreams, repeating time and again that the world has meaning, order, and purpose, that man has meaning, direction, and purpose. Larue expresses this eloquently:

> To know to whom one belongs, to sense poetically a heritage, to be linked emotionally and perhaps physically to a tradition rooted in antiquity and marked by beauty and suffering, joy and heartache is to acquire psychic strength to meet the trauma of existence and to answer the absurdity of the human dilemma of man existing briefly in endless time and space. (1975, p. 201)

Confirming these views in his *Myth and Disease,* Sam Keen (1977) goes so far as to suggest that the myths we live inform our organism, direct its choice of disease and even its style of dying (though not, of course, its cause).

"The Abyss of Meaninglessness"

If modern man were capable of fully facing "the abyss of meaninglessness" (Jung, 1958, pp. 72-73) which would result from the absence of myth, hence of meaning, his despair would spur him either to commit suicide–the only logical course of action, according to Camus (1961)–or to generate some new projection to fill the unbearable void. Paraphrasing Voltaire's comment on man's need for the idea of God, one could say that "If myth did not exist, it would have to be invented." Fortunately, wherever man is, there is myth. Granted, modern man lives in a world immensely different from that of earlier generations. But his need-system, his basic nature has not changed: "The psyche is ancient." (Jung, 1971, p. xxi) Consequently, modern man, like his archaic counterpart, needs guidance from an organized set of beliefs. Like his forbears, he tends to become emotionally upset whenever these beliefs are challenged or denied. He does not, indeed, cannot regard his myth as a guiding fiction–existentially often trustworthy and beneficial but, nevertheless, even at its best, an historically-determined interpretation, a serious type of fiction.*

---

*Incidentally, myth–though essentially fictitious–is apt to provide cues that may spur or guide intellectual endeavor, as is occasionally born out in the case of medieval and biblical myths which provide hints that guide archeologists in, for instance, locating and identifying certain sites, interpreting "the crossing of the Red Sea," or Joshua's "arresting the sun" at the siege of Jericho. (Roberts, 1976)

PART TWO

The Myth of the Scientific Worldview

1. The Master-Myth

Leading all other modern myths currently competing for adoption as a worldview is the Myth of the Scientific Worldview, a collective system of beliefs pervading not only academia but, with varying degrees of awareness and sophistication, all segments of society. Connecting science with myth may seem, at first glance, offensive, a contradiction in the terms, indeed, iconoclastic. Isn't science precisely that chastening, painstaking endeavor which strips the mind of its mythic proclivities? The question betrays an obsolete concept of myth as a confabulation when actually, in the present meta-mythological context, myth represents the very crystallization of the dominant values, aspirations and beliefs of a culture at a particular phase of its development. In fact, the belief that science stands outside of man's mythmaking urge is itself a significant element of the myth–which accounts for the vigor of its hold on modern society.

Not Science Per Se

Though my topic seems clearly enough stated in the title, I should nevertheless hasten to emphasize that—in deference to the very myth in question—I am referring not to science *per se*, its practice, methods, representatives and, especially, its applications which enhance our daily lives in countless ways. Science is undeniably impressive and justly honored. It is the glory of "the questing beast" at the current stage of his evolution. Granted, the *use* of certain scientific findings is questionable (when not outright destructive). But the findings themselves, the intelligence and disciplined effort involved in acquiring them, command unconditional respect.

What I am referring to, then, is not the scientific enterprise itself but the rhetoric, the ideology, indeed, the mystique which surrounds science and its achievements. Such a mystique was bound to develop, considering the spectacular character of scientific and technological achievement, crowning more than two centuries of predictions about science as the salvation of mankind. Also implied in this myth is the assumption that only those questions are worthy of concern that can be answered by the particular procedure called scientific.

As for that other weasel-word of the above title, "modern,"* it too deserves clarification. For this, Eliade's definition adequately serves my purpose:

> By the "modern world," we mean contemporary Western society; but also *a certain state of mind* which has been formed by successive deposits ever since the Renaissance and the Reformation. The active classes of the urban societies are in this sense "modern"—that is,

---

*Eliade's broad definition of modern man differs from—and is in fact almost opposed to—the very restricted sense in which another leading scholar on myth defines this concept. (Jung, 1933, pp. 226-228)

the mass of mankind which has been more or less directly shaped
by education and official culture. (1957, p. 25; italics added)

Modern, then, refers to a way of "being-in-the-world"
(Heidegger, 1962), as well as to the particular time-span during
which the scientific worldview developed toward its peak–now
distinctly passed, as evidenced by the stream of publications
from eminently credible observers of the contemporary world
scene who expose, criticize, and denounce that worldview–and,
in many cases, even science itself. For society at large, however,
the upward trend of the myth's popularity is still vigorous–which
is what counts where the social-philosophical and the political
import of myth is concerned.

Does the Scientific Worldview Truly Qualify as Myth?

Having singled out this particular worldview as the *master-
myth* of modern society, the question arises: Can such validly
be done–or is this merely a manifestation of the tendency, rife
among scholars of myth, to discern sometimes farfetched
parallels? To determine if the term *myth* may be legitimately
applied to modern man's attitude toward science, we must check
the issue against the criteria of myth enumerated earlier.

First, is it at all conceivable that the emancipated,
disenthralled man of our time should slip into mythic thinking?
The question reveals, once more, a concept of myth as an inferior
mode of thinking when, actually, mythic thinking is unavoidable
where man is faced with the unknown–which he is at every step
of his ascent toward fuller "hominization" (Teilhard de Chardin,
1965, p. 180). For he is always faced with futurity and, for a
long time to come, with the mystery of life (at least in its highest
forms). Wherever a dominant *collective* orientation and body of
beliefs develops about the unknown, we have myth. Authorities
on the subject agree unanimously that there is "no reason to

believe that the myth-forming processes of the last ten thousand years have differed materially from modern myth-making processes." (Boas, 1916, p. 879) Jung's position is even more fundamental: "Nothing," he writes, "goes to show that primitive man thinks, feels, or perceives in a way that differs fundamentally from ours." (1933, p. 148) True, modern conceptual thinking is more articulate, more differentiated and better informed, but the constitutive processes and categories of thinking have remained the same. Realizing the truth of these statements may be difficult:

> we are so much a part of our modern mythic environment that we usually fail to perceive it. It has, in a sense, environed us and it has become a projection of the self, just as it has helped to shape the self. (Larue, 1975, p. 4)

The Structure is Ancient

Proceeding to the *structure* of the myth in question, we learn from Larue (1975) that modern myths exhibit the very same formal characteristics as found in the most ancient type of myth, the Mesopotamian; namely, that of a primordial opposition between the two forces, light and dark, day and night, good and evil, hero and villain. In keeping with this traditional pattern, the myth of the scientific worldview pits knowledge against ignorance, proof against superstition—or what is perceived as being all these.

Can it further be said of the scientific worldview that it is "emotionalized"—which it must also be to qualify and function as myth? At first glance, no. Science is neutral, dispassionate, detached, unbiased. So indeed it aims to be. However, this serene atmosphere describes not science itself but the cultish climate of beliefs which surrounds science. The climate in which science actually develops is, in reality, far from being unemotional. Not only the politics of science (Snow, 1954) but also its very practice involve emotion. Even scientists of similar persuasion, engaged in the same pursuits, are apt to generate almost as much heat as light, as revealed, for instance, in James Watson's (1968) first-hand account, *The Double Helix*, and Arthur Koestler's historical report, *The Sleepwalkers* (1968). Similarly, those who ascribe to the scientific worldview, who live it, tend to regard their opponents as naïve, benighted or reactionary. They may treat them with condescending tolerance, even kindness—though not seldom with an undertone of derision or contempt. Students witnessing the jousts are apt to be intense and scornful on the subject, while most of their academic elders decline even to bother with the "medieval" notions of those who contend that, say, the logical positivist's net is too coarse to catch all that is contained in the ocean of potential knowledge. Though regrettable, these attitudes are understandable, considering that live myth is perceived as truth or oriented toward the truth, hence as holding—that is, entitled to hold—"always, everywhere and for everybody."

As for the requirement of collectivity, there is no doubt but that it is satisfied: "Science...has become a total culture dominating the lives of millions...." (Roszak, 1969, p. 216) It is not only the model, the pride and the product of modern society, it is its very "intercom," as Roszak calls it. Science generated a peaceful revolution and, as Reiff remarks, "genuine revolutions are basically religious in character." (Reiff, in Murray, 1960, p. 256) It presents us with a new world, and as Kerenyi (Jung and Kerenyi, 1963, p. 7) observes, "a new world is always born with a new god." (For a graphic example of this, think of the "Goddess" of Reason enthroned in Paris at the time of Rationalism.) While today's society is allergic to "gods" and "goddesses," it is quite able, willing and, indeed, eager to recognize as predicted by Taine (1889) and Saint-Simon (1760-

1825, Markham, ed., 1952), that science is the religion of the day.

Since myth arises from the meeting of the compulsion toward meaning with striking experiences and events, it follows that achievements as spectacularly prestigious and successful as science and technology must generate mythic generalizations. Such is a lawful and predictable process. It is interesting to note here that Emerson, as far back as a hundred years ago, noted in his journal that "a modern *mythology* would have to be industrial, mechanical, parliamentary, commercial, and socialistic...." (Levin, in Murray, 1960, p. 108; italics added)–a remarkably articulate prediction and, literally, borne out.

One last criterion remains to be checked before concluding that the scientific worldview fulfills indeed the nature and function of myth. It has to do with that transcendent quality designated as "religious in an extended sense." In the case of modern myth, this aura derives not from any notion of supernatural agency, but from the experience of science as something so strong, powerful, and real that it somehow achieves transcendent status. This image of scientific knowledge is one thing which modern society perceives unanimously, for it associates science with technology to the point of identifying the two: Since technology *works*, it is indubitably real; therefore scientific knowledge must also be real. The common man and even, it seems, certain academics, do not know that technology can work without its theoretical foundations having to be correct.

In connection with the cultish character of modern man's attitude toward science, it is amusingly revealing that contemporary language borrows so blithely from the vocabulary of the sacred to dramatize "Sci-Tech's" achievements. Such labels as "wonder-drugs," "miracle foods," and "Magic" you-name-its have become household words. Not only mercenary agencies but even the highest officials are apt to use the language of the sacred—as when a former U.S. president proclaimed that a human foot touching the surface of the moon "was to be ranked as the greatest thing since—Creation." (Trippett, 1977, p. 72)

From this brief review of the criteria of mythic status, it appears that the scientific worldview does qualify as myth, hence that it commands all the power to influence the behavior and psycho-social mood of those who incarnate the culture.

Is it Life-Affirming?

So far, we have only checked the formal requirements of mythic status, not its qualitative orientation. We have to ask: Is the scientific worldview humanly progressive or regressive? Does it tend to unify experience so as to generate constructive meaning, provide harmony, and foster the survival of man as the symbolic animal?

A glance at the contemporary world scene should set the stage for an answer. Both the scholarly observer and the man in the street agree that the world is in a state of tension and tumult so intense as to approach chaos or disintegration. The peculiar, paradoxical state of "chronic crisis" that marks our time is reflected in the sinister kind of epithets it has earned as: the Age of Confusion (Krutch, 1954, p. 15), of Anxiety (Auden, 1946), of Alienation (Terkel, 1974), of Anomie (Durkheim, 1951 [1897]), while its people are described as Sick (Tanzer, 1971), Aquisitive (Tawney, 1927), Lonely (Riesman, 1956), Angry (Pinter, 1965, 1968), Encapsulated (Royce, 1964), Apathetic (May, 1969, especially pp. 27-33), Transient (Toffler, 1970, pp. 45-76), One-Dimensional (Marcuse, 1964).

If the scientific worldview is indeed the master myth of this age, then this state of affairs hardly speaks in favor of its life-affirming value. The authentic myth unifies experience, enhances the meaning of life, and energizes man for effortful striving. Instead, the current scene exhibits all the deleterious effects entailed by the *in*authentic type of myth—the type that fails to satisfy the emotional undercurrent of the human need to understand and come to terms with things. This is not to say, however, that this myth is the one and only cause of the malaise of our time. It is emphasized because it pertains to the topic under discussion, myth and modern man. Technology, finance, economics, industry, the military, academia, Madison Avenue, Hollywood, the media contribute heavily to the shaping of the world scene.

Within this play of adverse forces and its unfortunate outcome, what can justifiably be charged to the scientific worldview? Before attempting to answer this question, we will pass in brief review two coordinate myths of the master myth of our time, namely the myth of objectivity and the myth-of-no-myth.

2. The Myth of Objectivity

In its pursuit of knowledge, science invests its highest value in a mode of knowing that is, ideally, impersonal and detached. Focused solely upon the *object* of inquiry and aiming to exclude all contamination by the inquiring agent, this approach is legitimately called objective. And where the object of the inquiry is non-human, such an approach is commendable and fruitful—as far as it reaches. But it does not reach nearly as far as the scientist wishes it would and the layman assumes that it does. Indeed, the key operations of science-in-the-making are essentially a function of the scientist. Hypothesis-forming, as we have it from Einstein himself, is almost mysteriously subjective. Similarly the interpretation of results and the formulation of conclusions are necessarily done by human agency. As Polanyi (1974) puts it, "knowledge is personal" and as Bridgman, the father of operationism, long confirmed, "we never get away from ourselves." (1959, p. 6)

These limitations of objectivity are not usually emphasized (or even mentioned) in the typical class or text, much less by popular works on science. On the contrary. *Objective* is made to convey unequivocally favorable meaning, referring to knowledge presumed to be trustworthy, verified, rational, tested, sanctioned, established, indeed, knowledge that is true and real. *Subjective*, on the other hand, is used synonymously with biased, emotional, distorted, insignificant, unreliable, idiosyncratic: a type of knowledge unworthy of being taken seriously because it emanates from the subject, not from the team or the hardware. The aura of value surrounding the former and the suspicion attached to the latter of these concepts account for the shaping of subtle but unmistakable collective attitudes with regard, not only to method, but to man himself, his capacity and worth.

These attitudes prevail not only in academia; they are found at all levels of education. People are made to admire and imitate this kind of approach—even though (and, perhaps, because) they understand little about the meaning, reach, and limits of objectivity. The aim proper of objectivity is, of course, truth—an attempt to reduce the observer's "personal equation" to a minimum. However, in the process of generalizing the objective approach to the realm of interpersonal behavior, aims and means get mixed up with one another, and objective detachment becomes "functionally autonomous" (Allport, 1961, p. 226)– being adopted for its own sake. "Objectivity as a state of being fills the very air we breathe in a scientific culture; it grips us subliminally in all we say, feel and do." (Roszak, 1969, p.216) It has become the commanding style of our age.

Consequently, the myth of objectivity, like all living myths, is regarded as the only sensible, valid stance, when actually the evidence that "there is no such thing as objectivity" (Polanyi,

1974), even in the physical sciences, is abundant, as Kuhn (1965), Bridgman (1959), Heisenberg (1979) and numerous others have argued—and demonstrated. The imperative of objectivity is, therefore, bound in many instances to violate direct experience. But this is no obstacle to its subjugating power. For it is possible through deletion and distortion to define things in such a way as to meet the criteria of objectivity. Better, one can change the experiencing subject:

> Even if it is not, indeed, possible to be objective, it *is* possible [and this precisely is the power of myth] so to the shape the personality that it will feel and act *as if* one were an objective observer and to treat everything that experience presents to the person in accordance with what objectivity would seem to demand. (Roszak, 1969, p. 216)

Although the myth of objectivity has, so far, resulted in relatively benign effects, it has nevertheless truly Orwellian possibilities. This is observable in countless instances, many of them innocuous but revealing of the myth's hold on contemporary society.

A typical instance of this uninvolved objectivist attitude in everyday life is the sophisticate's evaluation of art, especially in its dramatic or representational forms. His commentary on films, for instance, often pertains solely to the technical, purely visual or intellectual aspects of the production: lighting, effective close-ups, double-takes, flashbacks, and other clever manipulations of the film *Blow-Up* are a good case in point. Without seeing the film, one could never surmise from such comments that the plot involves eminently human issues. The fashionable viewer or critic cannot or dare not open himself to the effect of encounters with life and people. His response is typically confined to one dimension, the sensory dimension of the play of shadows on the screen.

This inability for symbolic participation in the enchantment, the awe, the ethical and emotional impact of the story, is particularly striking where distinctly romantic themes are concerned. Critics are not content simply to rate this kind of film a (perhaps realistic) low-C for creative or artistic value. They must scorn the thing wholesale, despite its sometimes searing human content–quite likely because of it. Conversely, many are apt to exalt the merits of such outrageously objectivist works as *Last Year at Marienbad* (Robbe-Grillet, 1962), which portray empty, robot-like characters sleepwalking through intimate encounters universally regarded as peaks of emotion. That the film aims to depict precisely the condition from which the viewer suffers is entirely overlooked.

Schorer's remark that literature, without adequate myths, models and images, degenerates into mere description makes a perverse sort of sense here: "When we feel that we are no longer in a position to say *what* life *means*, we must content ourselves with telling *how* it *looks*." (Schorer, in Murray, 1960, p. 357; italics added) True, this detached and scornful attitude toward romantic themes is not descriptive of the masses. But similar attitudes of hard-eyed observation are found in regard to other themes, e.g., invasion of privacy and, especially, violence, to wit Stanley Kubrick's *A Clockwork Orange* (on Anthony Burgess' [1963] vision of the future) is regarded as an illustration of the current societal chaos. While it would be hard to demonstrate the direct filiation of such attitudes and behavior from the impassive stance of scientific inquiry, the parallelism is thought-provoking. It seems hardly farfetched to assume that the indiscriminately investigative and analytical practice of science is not unrelated to the impoverishment of emotion and participative-capacity on the part of producers and consumers of art whose gratuitous witnessing is apt to be "more sadistic than participative." (Rieff, in Murray, 1960, p. 270)

In a lighter vein and by way of concluding the subject, an excerpt from Edwin Newman's humorous report (1976) on the present use of English—and of people—showing the extent to which manipulation is carried. He begins by explaining: "Sonorous design is produced by Muzak, the background...music company that calls its employees 'specialists in the physiological and psychological *applications* of music' and estimates that they *apply* it to 60,000,000 people a day." (p. 109, italics added) Newman emphatically declines having music "applied" to him and goes on to quote a gem of a statement from the company's program director, explaining that Muzak carefully avoids using any kind of music "for the purposes of entertainment," (p. 110) which reminds one of Walter Kerr's observation in *The Decline of Pleasure*:

> We are all of us compelled to read for profit, party for contacts, lunch for contracts, bowl for unity, drive for mileage, gamble for charity, go out for the evening for the greater glory of the municipality, and stay home for the weekend to rebuild the house. (1962, p. 39)

One wonders, with some concern, about the kind of fun the dawning Age of Leisure holds in store for the fully programmed citizen of the future.

3. The Myth-of-No-Myth

The most insidious element of the master-myth is the myth-of-no-myth, as May calls it. More perhaps than a part, this myth represents the crystallization, the shorthand version, of the myth of the scientific worldview.

Modern man quite typically thinks of himself as standing outside of myth, as liberated from indoctrination into belief-systems about his kind and his universe. More radically, he assumes that he has outgrown, not solely religious belief, but the very function of belief. His attitude is one of "show me" or "prove to me." Actually, the position that everything can be proved in a sense-perceptible and/or rational mode is itself based upon beliefs–powerful and often unexamined beliefs imbedded in one's assumptions. It does not occur to modern man that he has merely exchanged the myths of his forbears for contemporary, rationally more satisfying, or at least, more articulate ones. He is firmly entrenched in the myth-of-no-myth generated by the scientific worldview.

This attitude is, of course, readily understandable. Man's perennial attempt to make sense out of the complexity of self and the world is severely taxed at the present juncture. Tradition is all but abolished. Seasoned myths, most of them religious, that for generations used to give direction and meaning to human existence are badly battered, even outright eclipsed, by the secular orientation. New answers and solutions must be found to all the questions that assail him, the old as well as the new. Granted, he is no longer systematically indoctrinated, but he is heavily exposed to outside suggestions and disguised conditioning–while being deluded into believing he freely chooses his own answers.

The new world he faces is characterized, on the one hand, by mindboggling complexity; on the other, by the presence of countless specialists who seem to have "the" answer to any question or problem. A paradoxical world where everything appears at the same time impenetrable, yet stripped of all mystery. All the answers are on file–they only need retrieval and decoding by the expert. The questing beast is becoming the laboratory animal.

As passivity, intellectual docility, and apathy creep upon modern society, so does confusion. A proliferation of would-be myths, sundry theories and doctrines that vie with one another for the status of myth–that is, for the power and prestige of teachings that are "true always, everywhere, and for everybody"– these would-be myths succeed their rivals at a confusing rate reminiscent of the world of future shock (Toffler, 1970), where the pace of life is gauged by the speed with which things, first experienced as shocking, come to be felt as commonplace.

Consistent with his clinging to the myth-of-no-myth, contemporary man has a curious obsession with demythologizing. He does not realize that demythologizing is no longer possible; that consciously recognized (and, therefore, already devitalized) myths can only be desacralized or secularized–if they are the sort involving gods, goddesses or otherwise supernatural agency. Old myths wane and die, as new ones rise and grow to fill the existential vacuum, but deliberate mythoclasm tends to be followed by hasty and brittle remythologization.

To do away with myth as an essentially unconscious collective system of interpretation, man himself would have to be stripped of his "mythopoeic" (mythmaking) need. But this need being part of his basic nature, such is unlikely to occur before the felicitous "Omega Point" (Teilhard de Chardin, 1965) of mankind's evolution is reached. In the meantime, "the persistent belief that one truth invalidates the other," is according to Helen Luke, "at the heart of all our problems" (e.g., Luke, 1993).

PART THREE

Effects Upon the Individual and Society

Attempts to assess the psycho-social effects of these myths yield a less than rosy picture. While the current state of affairs is obviously not the result of a single set of factors, fairness to science *per se* demands that the multiplicity of causes be underscored. Fairness also demands recognition of the constructive forces that have simultaneously emerged, many of which are also related to science, e.g., a growing concern for ecology; for the protection of health; for the rights of minorities, including those of children; a recognition of the needs of the old, the handicapped, the dying. Nevertheless, at the present juncture, the effects on society of the forces of integration are not matching those of deterioration.

1. "The Well-Adjusted Man Without Problems"

A glance at the overall picture of the world in which the individual must find his moral sustenance may set the stage for the assessment. As Maslow sketches it:

> Every age but ours has had its model, its ideal. All of these have
> been given up by our culture; the saint, the hero, the gentleman,
> the knight, the mystic. About all we have left is the well-adjusted
> man without problems, a very pale and doubtful substitute. (1968,
> p. 5)

The "well-adjusted man without problems" is itself part of
the mythic system of our times, namely of the psychiatric myth.
According to Schorer (in Murray, 1960, pp. 355-356): "A
basically disorganized society such as ours is the result of a
number of antithetical and competing mythologies." And Larue
confirms:

> The present age may be viewed as a period of estrangement and
> disintegration—estrangement because many individuals have
> become acutely aware of their aloneness, of the unique personal
> identity that separates them from their fellow man in the vast abyss
> of the universe: disintegration because mythically sustained values
> are in the process of being broken down. (1975, p. 204)

Deprived of stable sources of existential meaning, modern man
predictably becomes disturbed. Hence our age is appropriately
described by the negative epithets cited above and borrowed
from the titles of leading psycho-social publications.

While modern man may not make the connection between
his crisis-state and the absence of a suitable worldview, he cannot
escape the realization that his pursuit of happiness, his search for
peace and contentment, is astoundingly unrewarding even though
the goods and privileges—freedom, health, wealth, leisure, education—
commonly regarded as the ingredients of happiness, are his to an
unprecedented extent. But ignorant and contemptuous as he is of
non-positivistic explanations, he tends to attribute the
meaninglessness, frustration, and anxiety which creep up on him
as due to some particular failure or deficiency in himself—his physical,
social, or sexual functioning, and the like. More frequently, he

situates the cause in the conditions of his environment, past or present: his upbringing, marriage or occupation–all of which are more likely to be effects rather than causes.

Goaded by the psychiatric spin-off of the myth of the scientific worldview, modern man typically takes his predicament to a therapist. In principle, a health-related agency may be just the place to contact. It has indeed been said repeatedly that "the diseases and crises of modern societies are rightly attributable to the absence of a mythology appropriate to them." (Eliade, 1957, p. 25) Unfortunately, the current training of therapists is such that all but a few are themselves inextricably caught in the same predicament as their clients. Hence the outcome of the treatment may mean adjustment to the prevailing impasse.

This unwitting capitulation of man in the face of the scientific worldview represents actually a regression–not only for the individual but also for society. In Jung's words:

> The materialistic views of our day have a tendency which we can discern in archaic thought. Both lead to the conclusion that the *individual is a mere resultant*; in the first case, he is the resultant of natural causes, and in the second, of chance occurrences. According to both accounts, human individuality is nothing in its own right, but rather the accidental product of forces contained in the objective environment. This is through and through the archaic conception of the world according to which the single human being is never considered unique, but always interchangeable with any other and easily dispensable. By way of a narrow view of causality, modern materialism has returned to the standpoint of archaic man. But the materialist is more radical, because he is more systematic, than primitive man. The latter has the advantage of being inconsistent." (Jung, 1933, pp. 170-171; italics added)

The advantage means that he is to some degree open and, hence, apt to glimpse beyond the confining circle of modern science's positivistic orientation and indoctrination.

2. Diminished Man

Prominent among the effects of the myth of the scientific worldview would seem to be "a downgrading of man." (Rieff, in Murray, 1960, p. 249) A downgrading which results in a loss of faith in himself as a unique and eminently capable being who can and must take responsibility for himself in all matters affecting his immediate and long-term well-being. People have *typically* come to adopt the habit of looking to others instead of inside themselves for answers to their questions, both trivial and essential. This dependency is observable in the public's effortless capitulation before the specialist's pronouncement. A striking case in point is the docility—sometimes the eagerness—with which clients accept depth-psychological interpretations that may be dramatically opposed to their experience and may, moreover, vary significantly from analyst to analyst. (The alternative, namely, to resist these interpretations, would be diagnosed as "further evidence of their 'neurosis'.") The same attitude reveals itself in the apathy and existential passivity of our otherwise hyperactive society and in the blunting of people's capacity for puzzlement and wonder. As Fromm remarks in *The Forgotten Language*:

> Whatever the merits of our high degree of literacy and universal education, *we have lost the gift for being puzzled. Everything is supposed to be known*—if not to ourselves then to some specialist whose business it is to know what we do not know. In fact, to be puzzled is embarrassing, a sign of intellectual inferiority.... To have the right answers seems all-important; to ask the right questions is considered insignificant by comparison. (1951, p. 3; italics added)

Denouncing this one-sided eagerness for "the right" answers is, of course, not to decry the practice of consulting all valuable sources of information, books, charts, indices, and experts.

Whenever decisions must be made about practical, physical-technical matters and, to some degree, even personal ones, such a practice is commendable and often indispensable. But the advice obtained must be weighed against and integrated with the givens of experience, intuition, and personal affinities. What is to be deplored is the passive adoption of the proposed solutions, especially in matters as eminently personal as sex, marriage, parenthood, education, ethics, and religion, even leisure–all of which are increasingly patterned upon information or models supplied by external agencies. From lifestyle to *Weltanschauung* modern man, like the citizen of the *Brave New World* (Huxley, 1950), is being monitored by anonymous outside forces. Precisely this faith in the externals of life has had the effect of making man think less highly of himself.

To the doleful list of epithets earned by our times might rightly be added "The Age of Diminished Man."

3. Reducing Persons to Products

Related to the forces that engineer the downgrading of man is a powerful strand of influence emanating from academic psychology. It consists not in the use but in the emphasis placed upon animal and machine models for the explanation of human behavior, learning and motivation. Such models are useful for the study of elementary forms of behavior. But their generalization to complex, specifically human behavior amounts to a blatant reduction of persons to products–devoid of all autonomy. Such practices represent a typical case of amputating the object of study to fit the available method. This elimination of the actively conscious, deliberating and choosing self as a responsible determinant of behavior is apt, if unchecked, to entail serious consequences for society as well as for the individual.

Another instance of the process of devaluation of man is found in the apparently innocuous, indeed, "educational" offerings, via the mass media, of those ethological and psychological research films on chimps, apes, lions (a cast that always and understandably fascinates the viewer) showing the animals' elementary capacities for learning, caring, or social organization. The commentary and epilog which cap these kinds of films typically emphasize the "unsuspected weight and promise" of such research with reference to human nature and potential. Not only the unredeemed seriousness of those remarks, but the tone of voice in which they are uttered, convey an awe and reverence such as befits a confrontation with models for human emulation.

True, such commentary may, for one thing, he staged by the producer. For another, it may be aimed at justifying the money received in support of the research and especially, at obtaining further funding. But what is subliminally communicated to the public is that man's uniqueness is illusory; furthermore, that he can expect fundamental insights for the understanding and conduct of his life from the study of infra-human organisms.

That the message is effectively received is apparent from remarks frequently heard from students who have seen those films, either on commercial channels or as part of psychology courses. Their sometimes passionate resistance to the notion of the uniqueness of man, notwithstanding the all-enveloping evidence of his culture-building, toolmaking, lawmaking capacities, of his linguistic, scientific, artistic, technological achievements—in all of which the objectors are immersed and participating—that resistance seems ominous at times.

In conclusion, frequent and, as it were, competitive comparisons of the characteristics and capacities of man with those of sub-human organisms and non-human systems rob him of his "pride of place" (Rieff, in Murray, 1960, p. 249)–not at the center of the universe (a symbolic position which has no bearing on his worth and destiny) but as the leading and therefore responsible figure on the phylogenetic scale. The myth of the scientific worldview divests the human being of the humble pride he can take in being a "reed,…but…a thinking reed." (Pascal, 1958, p. 97)

4. Substituting I-It Connections for I-Thou Relations

Some of the pernicious effects of the myth in question can aptly be described in terms of Buber's concepts of I-Thou and I-It. There is, Buber argues (or should be), a radical difference between man's attitude toward others and his attitude toward things. In the former he *meets* a subject, a world of experience, thought, and feeling. In the latter, he *handles* insensate objects. The former situation results in *relations* between persons, the other in *connections* between things. In a personal relation, one subject, the I, approaches or encounters another subject, the Thou. In an I-It connection, only one center of awareness is involved; one center, the subject, observes, arranges, and manipulates the other, an object. These two attitudes represent the basic forms of interaction in which people are engaged. The former represents the world of *community*, the latter, the world of *organization*.

The pertinence of the I-It attitude to scientific investigation is easy to see. The scientist's carefully cultivated detachment toward the object of his inquiry is appropriate, productive, indeed, indispensable. At first glance, one may wonder why an attitude so fruitful in the laboratory becomes so harmful when carried over into everyday life—especially where nature and man are concerned. This can be answered in terms of a distinction made by Adler (in a different context) between the methodological and the ontological point of view. Methodologically, detachment, neutrality, or the agent-to-object attitude is the *sine qua non* of research—at least in the natural sciences. Not to adopt it in that context would defeat the purpose of the inquiry, would amount to anthropomorphizing and projecting. Ontological detachment, on the other hand, that is, detachment in regard to *being*, to reality at large, especially to people, aims at extracting the use-value of all things, sentient as well as insentient (but sentience-supporting). It leads to an alienation of the agent from others, the world and, ultimately, himself.

Need it be said that the I-It attitude did not wait for science to originate. Ruthless and unfeeling behavior is a timeless and probably systemic part of the human repertoire. However, there is little doubt but that the scale on which this attitude is currently implemented received a powerful boost from the celebrated (and misunderstood) notion of scientific objectivity.

PART FOUR

The Promise of Psychology

In this concluding section I will attempt to discern some emerging trends and potential developments which may portend for the future of man in his ongoing encounter with myth.

Modern man's pride in science and his deep attachment to the practical benefits it has brought him are most legitimate. At the same time (and quite independent of science *per se*), it is imperative to insist upon a less confined, humanly less sterile worldview than the one that has, unintentionally, been generated by science. Kerenyi states the case very well in his and Jung's *Essays on a Science of Mythology*:

> We can no longer dispense with the freedom from falsehood that true science confers upon us. What we demand besides this freedom, or rather demand *back* from science, is just this feeling of immediacy between ourselves and scientific subjects. (1963, pp. 1-2)

Already in the early 1930's Jung pointed to modern society's need and quest for a new myth, for an approach that "accepts modern scientific worldviews but holds that they are inadequate and do not comprehend the entire reality of the cosmos and of life." (1933, p. viii)

The dense fabric of hazy beliefs and attitudes which spins itself around man's awareness of the power and benefits of science proves harmful to his growth and survival as the questing, transcending, socio-ethical, in sum, as the symbolic animal. As we have seen, instead of unifying experience and promoting integration within self and world, the myth of the scientific worldview estranges him from both. It also contributes to a play of disruptive forces—technological, social, and psychological—resulting in a deep and world-wide malaise. Fortunately, inauthentic myths tend to be ineffectual, hence, relatively short-lived. A dramatic instance of their ephemeral fate is Alfred Rosenberg's notorious "Myth of the 20th Century." (Chandler, 1945)

1. Myth Forever?

A thoughtful confrontation with the nature of myth leaves one with the uncomfortable question: "Is mankind forever condemned to live within a mythic circle? Is there no exit to his hermeneutic prison? Is the size of the wheel the only variant of this symbolic treadmill?

The answer is *yes* and *no*. "Yes"[†], because myth is the response to an urge, an inexhaustible search built into the symbolic animal

---

[†]The words "yes" and "no" have been purposely reversed from what was found in the original draft. The decision to do so was based on the immediate and overall contexts in which the author is answering her own, negatively-phrased questions. She obviously intended the "open-ended" circle,

and aimed at an all-encompassing meaning with perfect fit. Therefore, mythmaking will endure, will continue to shape human thought and behavior. For the alternative to myth is absurdity: "Old myths die hard, but for some of us they do die and the absurdity of life obtrudes." (Larue, 1975, p. 211)

Over against this "yes" there is also a "no."[†] One based on the view that the circle may be open-ended, spiraling, either upward or downward–according to its effectiveness in meeting mankind's craving for consciouness-enhancing meaning. Indeed, the mythic nature of human thinking about the vast unknown may be eternal, but as earlier suggested, themes or contents change in the direction either of mankind's enhancement or downgrading. In connection with the next phase of the mythic evolution, a variety of positions is currently discernible. According to Larue:

> For some, one answer lies in laughter, in the recognition of the meaningless stupidity of all things and of the humor in the serious human effort to act as though there were some ultimate reality.... [However] Within the laughter there is a pathos, a deep sadness for the sickness of humans in their attempts to find themselves through the maze of living, a deep hurt at men's failures to achieve their human potential.... Among the scribes of this non-myth approach are William Faulkner, Donald Barthelme, and Kurt Vonnegut.

> [For others, however,] to laugh is to cop out. The alternative is to enter into serious dialogue, a continual wrestling bout with the absurd.... The absurdity may remain, but concerned involvement– and we return again to the much abused term *love*–is one way of living with the absurd. One commits oneself to doing, to reaching

---

the spiral, to be understood, not as a necessary "condemnation," but as a dynamic with *possibility* for life-affirming myth-making, a way out of a "hermeneutic prison." It is, therefore, assumed that she also would have reworded for clarification. (A.A.W.)

out, to touching, to empathetic involvement with the tragedies of existence and their absurdities.... Humans are...strengthened by concern and lifted through doing." (1975, p. 212)

A number of contemporary authorities belonging to a variety of fields support this focusing upon love as an alternative. Among the more articulate, Huston Smith affirms that "there is no questioning the effectiveness of [love for the] solution to man's dilemma"—but adds the realistic qualification that "the problem is to keep it working." (in Richardson and Cutler, 1969, p. 7)

And there are those in whom mythic loss produces a feeling of being loosened from their existential moorings. Their solution consists in "what has been called 'the leap of faith' which transcends intellectual analysis." (Larue, 1975, p. 200) They insist that the results of their commitment are real, satisfying, and life-giving. Hence they choose to remain within traditional mythic frameworks with one important difference; namely, their decision is motivated not by blind obedience nor fear of divine punishment but by arguments of reason and common sense such as the following:

> The validity of holding onto ancient myth and...concepts that have proven themselves effective and valid though several thousand years of human history should not be discarded. There can be no question that the past exerts a stabilizing effect on the present and provides continuity and solid, tested foundations for action. Experience has taught humans many lessons, and to reject lightly what man has learned and cherished could be the height of folly." (Larue, 1975, p. 201)

Consequently, Larue goes on, there will continue to be quite a few

> who will find personal identity through mythic tradition. Christians will recite the Lord's Prayer and the Apostles' Creed

without analysis and will sense a unity with millions of other Christians who have spoken the same words through two thousand years of human history. Jews will repeat the *Sh'ma* in the awareness that this statement of identity and faith has been associated with joy and tragic sorrow extending back to the sacking of Jerusalem by the Babylonians. (1975, p. 200)

Finally, there is a hybrid type of position that might be called existential neo-stoicism, held by the thoughtful few

who are fully aware that they are adapting ancient mythic themes to modern settings, and who will not be disturbed by the knowledge. They will live in the spirit of Wallace Stevens, who has written: 'The final belief is to believe in a fiction, which you know to be a fiction, there being nothing else. The exquisite truth is to *know* that it is a fiction and that you believe in it willingly. (Larue, 1975, pp. 200-201)

We must assume that the fiction Wallace Stevens had in mind was fiction in the sense of a truth. For even the most stoic among us could not believe in *mere* fiction. An attitude of this kind would be similar to the emerging view of science (not of course, technology) as a metaphor. (Fertile metaphor, indeed, but nevertheless, metaphor.)

2. "Psychic Life Survives Its Own Eclipse"

Contemporary man's concept of mankind and of human values is, as we have seen, at a low point. Fortunately, as Jung points out, "psychic life survives its own eclipse." (1933, pp. 241-242) The first, perhaps, to discern the signs of a revival was Jung himself who, as the analyst of spiritual man, foresees this revival in terms of an upsurge of repressed spiritual tendencies. Jung's translator, Cary F. Baynes, elaborates on Jung's observation:

The western world stands on the verge of a spiritual rebirth, that is, a fundamental change of attitude toward the values of life. After a long period of outward expansion, we are beginning to look within ourselves once more. There is a very general agreement as to the phenomena surrounding this *increasing shift of interests from facts as such to their meaning and value to us as individuals*, but as soon as we begin to analyze anticipations nursed by the various groups in our world with respect to the change that is to be hoped for, agreement is at an end and a sharp conflict of forces makes itself felt." (1933, p. vii; italics added)

In the face of a mythic process at once disintegrating and germinating, the presence of divergent views such as those just reviewed is unavoidable and, perhaps, fertile.

Among contemporary authors representing this concept of incipient spiritual rebirth are the contributors to the book, *Transcendence*. In his introduction to this work, Richardson points to the momentous fact of

a major intellectual opening in America—an opening that may mean *a more radical reorientation in outlook than the Enlightenment and the development of science,* more radical because it is more *dis*continuous with our past intellectual and spiritual traditions." (in Richardson and Cutler, 1969, p. xiii; italics added)

In stating that we live in an axial moment when man's questions as well as his answers are being reconstructed, Richardson expresses the feeling of a growing number of observers of the contemporary scene, who see that in some important sense the future of man is open and the outcome of life processes around us is contingent upon the action and/or spiritualization of man. In connection with this openness of the world, Kerenyi confirms:

If "cosmos" is understood in the Greek sense that everything spiritual and our compulsion towards the spiritual are an essential part of the cosmos, then here we have *the cosmos meeting with itself.**

> Or, to put it in more scientific language, it seems as if there already were in the human plasm—the germ of life we have been speaking of—something spiritual, a compulsion towards the spiritual." (Jung and Kerenyi, 1963, p. 21)

Considering the sway of current positivistic myths, with their exclusive focus upon the sensate, the tangible, and the material, it seems farfetched to assume that things are likely to change into their very opposite, namely from a denial to an affirmation of man's spiritual urges. Actually, appearances notwithstanding, the lawfulness of such reversals has long been recognized by culture-historians and philosophers. The ancient Greeks already had a name for it, the rule of *enantiodromia*, or conversion of a process into its opposite—a concept better known as Hegel's dialectical sequence of thesis, antithesis, synthesis.

An instance of such a reversal is found in the earlier mentioned emergence of love as the solution to the crisis resulting from the current, generalized state of alienation. For those who consider this a simplistic or sentimental point of view, Jung offers a line of thought of a different nature, more consonant with clearly visible trends at work in the current world. To this perspective we now turn.

3. The Promise of Psychology

In regard to the resolution of the human predicament, Jung suggests the momentous possibility that psychology might

---

*An idea expressed in almost identical terms by Teilhard de Chardin as "the universe becoming conscious of itself." (1965)

provide the next link in the evolution of man's striving for meaning, strength, and harmony. In Jung's view (1933) it is not mere curiosity that has led modern man to 'the discovery of psychology,' but spiritual need. In his own words:

> The rapid and world-wide growth of a 'psychological interest'...shows unmistakably that modern man has to some extent turned his attention from material things to his own subjective processes.... This 'psychological interest'... shows that man expects something from psychic life which he has not received from the outer world...(p. 237) [and that] *the crux of the spiritual problem of today is to be found in the fascination which psychic life exerts upon modern man.* (p. 251; italics added)

The fascination which psychology exerts upon 20th century Western man is a fact. It is unmatched by any wave of interest of a symbolic—that is, non-materialistic, non-physical—nature. This over-riding appetite for psychological enlightenment is reflected in the prodigious sale of books and the enrollment in courses on the subject. Even more, perhaps, in the nation-wide demand for psychological services. As for Jung's interpretation of this fact as a manifestation of a search for the spiritual, it is hard to dismiss by anyone observing the phenomenon at close quarters, such as teachers and therapists. Corroboration of Jung's hypothesis issues further from the simultaneous decline of religion (at least in its traditional manifestations), also from religion's heavy borrowing of psychological language, practices, and explanations. True, there are also signs of distinctly religious forms of revival, but they are sporadic, heterogeneous, and controversial, and cannot be compared to the tidal wave of interest in psychology.

What we are currently witnessing, then, is a double movement, one *toward*, the other *away from* concerns with what can be called ultimates such as: Who am I? What does it mean to be human? What is it that urges me on? What values are most worthy of pursuit? What does it mean to function fully? Do I have a real say in my destiny? Or, am I "operated" by forces over which I have no real control? What is the good life? How is it achieved? All these questions can be dealt with in either religious or psychological terms. They used to be answered by religion with far more definiteness, consolation, and comfort than psychology can offer. Yet people tend to turn to psychology for the satisfaction of the whole gamut of their spiritual needs—from a natural curiosity about the forces that stir within to a concern with the transcendent and metaphysical realms of thought.

Historical Threads

How are we to understand this shift of model in people's quest for understanding of the world of the invisible? Two lines of thought seem to account for the change. One is historical, the other lies in the congeniality between the modern temper and psychology's particular approach. In historical perspective, we find that the first phase of psychology's development (in the late 19ᵗʰ century) had little to do with any therapeutic, much less spiritual concerns—except, perhaps, in preparing the terrain for what was to follow. Indeed, the startling news of Wundt's "measuring" of psychological processes may have had a "subversive" or secularizing effect upon the traditional view of the psyche or soul as the divine spark. By itself, however, this "quantification of the unquantifiable" might have remained inconsequential if not for the advent of psychoanalysis.

Psychoanalysis

A mythic impetus clearly originated when psychoanalysis exploded upon the scene. Freud's concept of personality in terms of agencies—the id, ego, and superego—was unmistakably mythological in structure and function. In addition, these agencies were depicted in colorful and epic images. The vividness of their representation readily invited reification: The id as the cave-dwelling primitive, threatening to burst to the surface anytime; the ego evoking an insecure executive beset by demands, trying to placate at once the turbulent id, the stern and vengeful superego and also the rules of watchful reality outside—while trying to get in a little living of his own. Next to its sexual focus, the major reason for the strong impact of Freudian psychoanalysis lies precisely in the epic character of its canvas of vividly portrayed and competing protagonists, resembling the classical figures of gods, villains, and powerless mortals. The vitality and longevity of any myth is heavily dependent upon a suitable imagery and pageantry, as we learn from scholars of myth.

Self-Psychology

In a very different way, self-psychologies may also have contributed to the development of psychology as a step-stool toward spiritual concerns. Though free from the myth-inducing imagery of psychoanalysis, these psychologies focus attention upon the self as the subjective core of existence and reality, and as the center of creativity, autonomy, and hence, responsibility, all of which leads to concerns of a deeply philosophical nature directly related to spiritual concerns.

Behaviorism

Paradoxically, even behavioristic psychologies can be viewed as having contributed, however indirectly, to the new existential-philosophical orientation of psychology. In stripping man of his traditional belief in the reality of the "I" and its intellectual-volitional faculties, Behaviorism affected man's belief in the operation of any invisible, intangible agency whatever. This radically im-personal stance resulted in a psychological void—with its compelling urge for something to fill the vacancy. Thus, the "search for self" and "search for identity," so characteristic of the last few decades, can be seen as having served to remedy this reduction of man to mere reaction.

Humanistic Psychology

More directly responsible than any other theoretical strand of influence is probably humanistic psychology—in its scholarly reaches. The emphasis of this new psychology upon the unique, irreducible nature of man, upon the specific human capacities—for reflective thought (knowing that he knows), for declarative language (not simply communication) for devising symbols, laws, tools (tools that make tools), wills, games, in one word: culture, in its revelation of man as the only animal who exists, knowingly in space-time, who manifests transcendental and metaphysical concern throughout history and culture—all this opened perspectives that merge with other disciplines ranging from computer technology to philosophy and even religion.

Equally influential (though in a different vein) is the therapeutic strand of psychology ranging from psychoanalysis to the current encounter group movement. The emphasis of those endeavors upon the depth of experience and the expanding of awareness, upon honesty and authenticity, upon the validity of the emotional component of human existence, and the importance of sharing and communicating, upon love, trust, compassion, and empathy amounts, in the ideal case, to a rephrasing and enacting of the central tenets of the world's great religions.

Freedom From Boundaries

Perhaps the major appeal of the psychological path to the quest for ultimate value and spiritual nurturance is that it satisfies modern man's exacerbated need for freedom. Psychology, like man's curiosity and imagination, has no boundaries. Not suprisingly Comte (1830-1842; Andreski, ed., 1974) regarded psychology as the field of knowledge toward which all disciplines ultimately converge. Indeed, it can be expanded to include everything—in so far as knowledge of anything (animate or inanimate, past or present) exists only in so far as it is in human awareness. Consciousness and rationality merge with the boundless unconscious—not only the personal but also, according to Jung (Jung and Kewrenyi, 1963, pp. 71-74), the collective unconscious, that repository of experiential patterns of the human race dimly resonating through the individual organism.

Similarly–as we learn from recent findings in the biological sciences–experiences, thought, emotion, merge with the tissues, with their chemistry and biochemistry in ways that are increasingly observed, but whose actual "osmosis" remains as mysterious as ever. Even subatomic physics reveals aspects of the behavior of matter that evoke properties of the mind: movement as fast as thought (the neutrinos in the linear accelerator); penetration as deep as logic (X-rays and lasers); acceleration and bonding (the atoms of the molecule); and something like freedom in the indeterminacy of the particles– acting as if they had a mind of their own, bent upon resisting and escaping observation, yielding information about either their position or their velocity, but refusing to yield both simultaneously.

"Queerer Than We Can Suppose"

Scientific in origin though all these findings are, they convey an intense sense of mystery—which J.B.S Haldane summarized pointedly in quipping: "The universe is not only queerer than we suppose, but queerer than we *can* suppose." (1928, p. 298)

When pursued far enough and frankly faced, the mystery of human existence and of the universe as revealed by science is every bit as opaque as traditional theological teachings. However, it differs from the latter in two significant ways. The mysteries of the new universe are intimated via *discovery* and repeatable procedure. Those of religion are *imposed* by dogma. No form of learning is as pervasive, as joyful, as discovery—none as aversive (at least to moderns) as imposed truths. Second, the mystery involved in the new physics, the new biology, the new humanistic psychology is of a kind that invites, stimulates, indeed, promises ultimate disclosure. Conversely, the mysteries of traditional religion discourage, indeed, defy clarification.

CONCLUSION

From Code-Centered to Care-Centered

How does the outcome of the psychological path of spiritual search compare with traditional approaches to the spiritual?

At its best, and judging from the samples as yet available, the outcome is comparable to the essential teachings of the world's great religions, namely: a respect for self and for others—in all their differentness; a reverence for the vast unknown; an emphasis upon the values of truth, honesty, authenticity, responsibility; a delight in sharing, in accepting the fellow human being without distinction of externalia. But there is more. Unique values accrue from the very process of sharing, searching and striving. Indeed, the discovery of existential truth through personal interest and effort, and attempts at a lifestyle guided by these truths tend to make for a more mature attitude than ensues from passive submission to dogmatic creed and prescribed ritual. One of its merits is likely to consist in a more existential, more truly felt commitment to values freely espoused. Another one derives from the opportunity to explore one's intimations of the ultimate at a pace at which insight can be integrated with the totality of experience. To the passive (or, apparently passive) stance of religious adherence, it offers a more active, more creative and autonomous alternative, more in keeping with the modern temper. More active in that it allows the individual to be rationally as well as intuitively engaged in an attempt to satisfy both the intellect and the emotional undercurrents of understanding. The psychological approach is thus more creative in allowing the subject to start from his "subjective zero," from wherever it makes sense for him to start, leaving him free to define transcendental values and meaning in accordance with the progress of his understanding. More creative also because in the ongoing process of analyzing and integrating his experience, man creates himself .

Finally, with respect to the behavioral implementation of the insights and values thus glimpsed, it would seem that in the ideal case, the laws of social-ethical conduct would not need to be imposed upon the carefully—and caringly—self-scrutinizing individual. They could be derived from experiential feedback, that is, from man's capacity to examine his experience with regard to what "feels good," what "feels bad," in interpersonal relations, allowing him to discover the prime injunction of social-ethical behavior: "Do unto others...."

In sum: from code-centered, as it was traditionally, man's ethical makeup could become care-centered.

BIBLIOGRAPHY*

Adler, Mortimer J. *The Difference of Man and the Difference It Makes*. New York: Holt, Rinehart and Winston, 1967.

Allport, Gordon W. *Pattern and Growth in Personality*. New York: Holt, Rinehart and Winston, 1970.

Auden, W.H. *The Age of Anxiety*. New York: Random House, 1946.

Boas, Franz. "Tsimshian Mythology." In *U.S. Bureau of American Ethnology, 31ˢᵗ Annual Report, 1909-10*. Washington, D.C., 1916, pp. 29-1037.

Bridgman, Percival W. *The Way Things Are*. Cambridge, Massachusetts: Harvard University Press, 1959.

Buber, Martin. *I And Thou*. Translated by Walter Kaufmann. New York: Charles Scribner's Sons, 1970

Burgess, Anthony. *A Clockwork Orange*. New York: W.W. Norton & Company, Inc., 1963.

Camus, Albert. *The Myth of Sisyphus and Other Essays*. Translated from the French by Justin O'Brien. New York: Vintage Books, 1961.

Chandler, Albert R. *Rosenberg's Nazi Myth*. Ithaca, New York: Cornell University Press, 1945.

Comte, Auguste. *The Essential Comte*: Selected from *Cours de Philosophie Positive* (1830-1842). Edited by Stanislav Andreski; translated by Margaret Clarke. New York: Harper & Row Publishers, Inc., 1974.

Durkheim, Emile. *The Elementary Forms of Religious Life*. Translated by Joseph W. Swain. London: George Allen & Unwin Ltd., ©1915, 1957.

---

*There were quotations in the original draft for which only the authors' names were cited. In such cases where the exact quote could not be found, reference is made to pages in the authors' works where the *idea* expressed in the quote can be found. Professor Kinget may have been reading in the original foreign language versions of these works and differences in translation may account for these instances. *A.A.W.*

Durkheim, Emile. *Suicide: A Study in Sociology.* Translated by John A. Spaulding and George Simpson. Glencoe, Illinois: Free Press, 1951. (original publication 1897).

Eliade, Mircea. *Myth and Reality.* Translated by Willard R. Trask. New York: Harper & Row Publishers, 1963.

Eliade, Mircea. *Myths, Dreams and Mysteries.* Translated by Philip Mairet. London: Harvill Press, 1957.

Eliade, Mircea. *The Myth of the Eternal Return, or Cosmos and History.* Translated by Willard R. Trask. Princeton, New Jersey: Princeton University Press, 1965 (1949).

Frankl, Viktor E. *The Will to Meaning: Foundations and Applications of Logotherapy.* Cleveland, Ohio; The World Publishing Company, 1969.

Fromm, Erich. *The Forgotten Language.* New York: Rinehart & Co., Inc., 1951.

Gunkel, Hermann. *The Legends of Genesis: The Biblical Saga and History.* Translated by W.H. Carruth. New York: Schocken Books, 1964.

Haldane, J.B.S. *Possible Worlds And Other Papers.* New York: Harper & Brothers Publishers, 1928.

Heidegger, Martin. *Being And Time.* New York: Harper & Row, Publishers, 1962.

Heisenberg, Werner. *Philosophical Problems of Quantum Physics.* Woodbridge, Connecticut: Ox Bow Press, 1979. (Formerly Titled: *Philosophic Problems of Nuclear Science.* New York: Pantheon Books, Inc., 1952.)

Huxley, Aldous. *Brave New World.* New York: Harper's Modern Classics, 1950.

Jung, C.G. *Modern Man in Search of a Soul.* Translated by W.S. Dell and Cary F. Baynes. New York: Harcourt, Brace & Co., 1933.

Jung, C.G. *The Portable Jung.* Edited by Joseph Campbell; translated by R.F.C. Hull. New York: The Viking Press, Inc., 1971.

Jung, C.G. *The Undiscovered Self.* Translated by R.F.C. Hull. Boston: Little, Brown and Company, 1958.

Jung, C.G and Kerenyi, C. *Essays on A Science of Mythology.* Translated by R.F.C. Hull. New York: Harper & Row, 1963.

Keen, Sam. "Myth and Disease." An address given at the Forces of Life Conference, Plymouth, Michigan, April, 1977.

Kerenyi, C. *The Religion of the Greeks and Romans.* Translated by Christopher Holme. New York: E.P. Dutton & Co., Inc., 1962.

Kerr, Walter. *The Decline of Pleasure.* New York: Simon and Schuster, 1962.

Koestler, Arthur. *The Sleepwalkers.* London: Hutchinson & Co. Ltd., 1968.

Krupka, Lawrence A. *Michigan State University 1976-77 Academic Programs.*

East Lansing, Michigan: Michigan State Unversity Press, 1976, p. 93.

Krutch, Joseph Wood. *The Measure of Man.* New York: Grosset & Dunlap, 1954.

Kuhn, Thomas S. *The Structure of Scientific Revolutions.* Chicago: The University of Chicago Press, 1965.

Larue, Gerald A. *Ancient Myth and Modern Man.* Englewood Cliffs, New Jersey: Prentice-Hall, Inc., 1975.

Lang, Andrew. *Modern Mythology.* London: Longmans Green and Co., 1897; New York: AMS Press, 1968.

Levin, Harry. "Some Meanings of Myth." In Murray, Henry A., ed., *Myth And Mythmaking.* New York: George Braziller, Inc.,1960.

Luke, Helen. "The Way of Woman Ancient and Modern." Private publication. See the later publication, *Kalidescope: "The Way of Woman" and Other Essays.* New York: Parabola Books, 1993 (2nd Ed.).

Malinowski, Bronislaw. "Myth in Primitive Psychology." In *Magic, Science and Religion and Other Essays.* Boston, Massachusetts: Beacon Press, 1948.

Malinowski, Bronsilaw. *The Foundations of Faith and Morals.* London: Humphrey Milford, 1936.

Marcuse, Herbert. *One-Dimensional Man.* Boston, Massachusetts: Beacon Press, 1964.

Maslow, Abraham. *Toward a Psychology of Being.* Second edition. New York: Van Nostrand Reinhold Company, 1968.

May, Rollo. *Love and Will.* New York: W.W. Norton & Company, Inc., 1969.

Müller, Friedrich Max. *Contributions to the Science of Mythology.* London, New York and Bombay: Longmans Green, 1897.

Murray, Henry A., ed. *Myth and Mythmaking.* New York: George Braziller, Inc., 1960.

Newman, Edwin. *A Civil Tongue.* Indianapolis and New York: The Bobbs-Merrill Company, Inc., 1976.

Pascal, Blaise. *Pascal's Pensees.* New York: E.P. Dutton & Co., Inc., 1958.

Pinter, Harold. *The Birthday Party.* New York: Grove Press, 1968.

Pinter, Harold. *The Caretaker.* New York: Grove Press, 1965.

Polanyi, Michael. *Personal Knowledge.* Chicago, Illinois: University of Chicago Press, 1974.

Richardson, Herbert W. and Cutler, Donald R., eds. *Transendence.* Boston, Massachusetts: Beacon Press, 1969.

Rieff, Philip. "A Modern Mythmaker." In Murray, ed., *Myth and Mythmaking.*

Reisman, David. *The Lonely Crowd*. New Haven, Connecticut: Yale University Press, 1958.

Robbe-Grillet, Alain. *Last Year At Marienbad*. New York: Grove Press, 1962.

Roberts, Steven V. "Myth Proves a Factual Guide to Archeology." *The New York Times*, December 12, 1976, Sec. E, p.8

Roszak, Theodore. *The Making of a Counterculture*. Garden City, New York: Doubleday and Company, Inc., 1969

Royce, Joseph R. *The Encapsulated Man*. Princeton, New Jersey: D. Van Nostrand Company, Inc., 1964.

Saint-Simon, Henri. *Henri Comte De Saint-Simon (1760-1825): Selected Writings*. Edited and translated by F.M.H. Markham. New York: The Macmillan Company, 1952.

Schorer, Mark. "The Necessity of Myth." In Murray, ed., *Myth and Mythmaking*.

Snow, C.P. *The New Men*. New York: Charles Scriber's Sons, 1955.

Stauffer, Donald A. "The Modern Myth of the Modern Myth." In Wimsatt, W.K., ed. *Literary Criticism: Idea and Act*. Berkeley, California: University of California Press, 1974.

Strenski, Ivan, ed. *Malinowski And The Work of Myth*. Princeton, New Jersey: Princeton University Press, 1992.

Szasz, Thomas S. *The Myth of Mental Illness: Foundations of a Theory of Personal Conduct*. New York: Harper & Row, Publishers, 1974.

Taine, H.A. *On Intelligence*. Translated by T.D. Haze. New York: Henry Holt and Company, 1889.

Tanzer, Michael. *The Sick Society*. Chicago, Illinois: Holt, Rinehart and Winston, 1971.

Tawney, R.H. *The Acquisitive Society*. London: G. Bell and Sons, Ltd., 1927.

Teilhard de Chardin, Pierre. *The Phenomenon of Man*. Translated by Bernard Wall. New York: Harper & Row Publishers, Inc., Second Harper Torchbook Edition, 1965.

Terkel, Studs. *Working: People Talk About What They Do All Day and How They Feel About What They Do*. New York: Pantheon Books, 1974.

Trippett, Frank. "Science is No Longer a Sacred Cow." *Time Magazine*, March 8, 1977.

Toffler, Alvin. *Future Shock*. New York: Random House, Inc., 1970.

Tylor, Edward. *Primitive Culture*. London: John Murray; New York: G.P. Putnam's Sons, 1920.

Watson, James. *The Double Helix*. New York: Atheneum, 1968.